I NEED A MAN!

I Need a MAN!

FROM MS. INDEPENDENT TO MRS.

Vanessa Lynn

Parables Entertainment LLC

Copyright

Dedication

Dedicated to the *Ladies in Waiting*

He messages you; you message him, then *wait*.

He texted you; you texted him, then *wait*.

You go on date after date...then *wait*.

You buy the books, attend the workshops, read the blogs, then *wait*.

You join the gym, change your diet, color your hair, then *wait*.

You work on yourself, take up a hobby, then *wait* and *wait* and *WAIT*.

This *wait* has spanned days, weeks, months, years, and even decades.

During this *wait*, no matter how you smile, take the girl's trips, or have a fun night out, you feel unloved, *unpretty,* and undesirable. You're tired of hearing "Just *wait* on God," what do people think you've been doing? The truth is girlfriend, your *wait* has now become a WEIGHT.

My prayer is, within the pages of this book, your load will become a little *lighter.*

Vanessa Lynn

I Need a Man!

Ladies! Has your dating life consisted of:

- Mama's boys that need help?

- Married, noncommittal men or Caspers that "ghost" you?

- Perchance, you've had a loving relationship and sabotaged it.

- Are you a resident of *no man's* land? Meaning, no man has asked you out since Myspace?

Is marriage your true end goal? If yes, everything you've done in your dating life thus far should be erased, like your ex's phone number.

This book is aimed at single women who desire traditional marriage, where the MAN is the head of the household.

Desiring to be a WIFE, in this hook-up-culture, will be no easy task. I NEED A MAN will guide you through the murky waters of the dating jungle, on your journey from *Ms. Independent to MRS.*

PROCEED WITH CAUTION: If marriage isn't a goal and you don't NEED a man, and prefer open relationships, sister-wives, sugar-daddies, going-with-the-flow, friends-with-benefits, situation-ships, and independence, may the force be with you. There are plenty of books on those subjects. This isn't one of them.

About the Author Vanessa Lynn

For two decades, Detroit Motown native, author, and visionary Vanessa Lynn enjoyed a former career as a wedding consultant and venue owner. She professionally consulted and served well over a thousand engaged couples. That experience gave her a unique and realistic observation of love and marriage.

Vanessa is a natural matchmaker. In 2013 she co-founded, *Dating for Grown Folks,* a private Facebook group where mature singles from the ages of 35-up could meet and mingle. Swiftly, group members began seriously dating and several couples actually tied the knot!

In community missions, she has organized programs for women, seniors, prison inmates, and donation drives to aid the Flint water crisis, Hurricane Harvey, and the Midland flood. In 2020, she released a musical EP *Lil Queens (*TL Girlz*),* which was featured on Fox 2 News Detroit and Beautiful News in South Africa, for its anti-bullying message.

Vanessa is an Amazon bestseller. Her two popular published books are *Girl, Get Your Date Life Right,* and *...The Ultimate Urban Playwrights Guide.* . Her vast works: *Unequally Yoked, Affairs, Boss Lady, Fakers, and Church Girl* (contributing writer) have been sold in Walmart, Target, Best Buy, aired on BET (*Church Girl*), and streamed on Amazon Prime, Tubi TV, IMBD TV, and Pluto TV among others.

From 2012 to the present, Lynn provides writing classes, coaching, ghostwriting, and consulting services. She is devoted to her numerous projects involving the family, love relationships, and youth. Vanessa Lynn has two adult daughters and one grandson. They are the joy of her life!

Contents

Introduction - The Interview

INTRODUCTION -THE INTERVIEW

- "Dating sucks!"

- "There are no good men out there!"

- "I don't need a man."

- "I'm doing me."

- "My biological clock is ticking."

- "Men are intimidated by me."

- "I'm waiting on God!"

Sound familiar? Or perhaps you're a grown woman who has her stuff together, and you find yourself actively dating. Maybe you haven't been on a date since the "Class of '88" prom. You're in a relationship, fresh off a breakup or nasty divorce, are a hopeless serial dater, or in a "confuse-a-ship". Honestly, you're bitter, angry, heartbroken, or just plain fed up with what seems to be a lack of quality available men. I mean, you are a good catch (so you believe). You've got a decent career, solid morals, for all intents and purposes, you are a "dime piece"! So why are other women, like you, getting married, and you can't seem to catch a break? Remember this, for a man to settle down and marry, he must feel you are the best woman for HIM.

Ladies, you may be a great catch but, you just can't seem to move past the interview process. Truth is, you really want to skip this process and just get straight to the vows! You keep starting over with men because you're stuck in the interview process, which is DATING.

People who can't seem to find viable employment, give similar reasons for being single.

- Not enough jobs (men).

- Too competitive (7 to 1 ratio).

- Not enough quality jobs (men are no good).

- Never permanent (noncommittal).

Have you ever seen people seemingly less qualified than others consistently beat their more-skilled counterparts time and time again for a position? There is a reason for that. And there is a reason why women who may not be as attractive or accomplished as you, seem to get and keep men all the time. It's just like landing a good job. It depends on a few factors. Follow me for a minute; I'm going somewhere.

Who are you? Do you have a great resume, a great personality, and the skills and qualities the job requires? Often, you may not be the most qualified, but you have the most personality. That is what attracts employers.

You know where to look. The reason why some people cannot land a job is that they don't know where to look. There are so many places to look for a job other than Monster. Craigslist, newspapers, networking, asking friends, cold calling, and yes, the various internet sites. Using all these various resources of opportunity vastly widens your chance of landing a good job.

So now that you have submitted your resume, the employer shows interest and would like to schedule an interview (first date).

The Interview (first date)

This is your make-or-break moment. This is where you must show your charm, wit, personality, and experience so the employer sees you as an asset and not a liability. The interview is also the time you find out if the job is the right fit for you. During the interview, you should not only be concerned about the pay scale, but you should also check out the atmosphere of the new job, the job requirements, and the benefits. During the interview, you may conclude that you are not the right fit, the employer may pass on you, or the decision may be mutual. But sometimes, we settle out of the need for funds or companionship, therefore removing ourselves from better job opportunities. The truth is you are just tired of looking!

Sometimes, there are follow-up interviews with more team members (parents, friends) and perhaps even skills and assessment tests. Remember, the higher paying and more prestigious the job, the more rigorous the hiring process. The employer is taking a big risk hiring you, so they just want to be sure you are the right fit long-term.

The Rejection Letter

You passed all the tests, and the employer seemed very impressed by you. The person who interviewed you even smiled and gave hints that you were a shoo-in for the job. Suddenly, you get a letter with these words: "We have chosen a candidate that closely fits our needs. We will keep your application on file." Yes, they sure will keep it on file. You were a good candidate but, in their minds, there was someone better. You felt like this was the job for you, but it didn't work out. You went through a lot and now you are disappointed. You were so sure the job was yours that you stopped looking for other employment. Now you must start all over again. Then again, you may get an...

Offer Letter

You see the email come through with the company's name. You hold your breath as you open it. The first thing you see is: "Congratulations! We would like to officially offer you the position of David's Lady!" Not really, but perhaps Customer Service Supervisor. The letter then explains specifics of the job, such as work hours, pay, benefits, usually a boatload of paperwork, orientation, and start date. You are thrilled, elated, and excited, but also nervous. Starting a new job is always scary because while it looks good on the outside, usually once you get into the day-to-day work, you find out all the drama, corporate politics, and unfair practices that take place on the job. But you could love your job and be there for the long haul.

Temporary or Contract Work

Now, there is also another kind of offer, which is temporary or contract work. You are not a permanent employee of the company, but your job duties are the same. You are there temporarily to see if they want to hire you full-time before paying out so much in benefits and vacation time. So here you are, stuck in a job, but you don't have the official title. You could come in knowing that a position is a contract and that it will always be a contract. Once the contract is up, you are gone. But sometimes, you stick around, hoping the job will see your value and hire you full-time. Maybe they will or maybe they won't. But if you stick around and do the work, they will pay you; you just won't be an official employee. You just work for them.

Hopefully, I've painted a clear picture of the dating scene. It's not about there being no good men available; actually, there are plenty of available men that can't seem to find the right woman. Don't believe me? Ask any single man you know; you'll find he has the same complaints about women as we do about men.

Today's dating scene is complicated. Oftentimes, women are disheartened after failed relationships, broken engagements, multiple rejections, and divorce. Women who have never been "chosen" or even date often, adopt a feeling of rejection. You often wonder what is wrong with you—physically, mentally, or emotionally—because after all these years, no man has ever chosen you to be his wife. Society, friends, other women, talk shows, books, and even religious institutions are all screaming in your ear, telling you how to handle your singlehood. Quite frankly, most of this advice is bad and harmful. Some modern women's movements imply that traditional marriage is outdated, and I've even heard it referred to as slavery! You don't have to be religious to understand there is something divine about a loving marriage.

For this journey, we are going to be real with ourselves and acknowledge our feelings and desires so that we can finally connect with your King. Now, pump your brakes! Before you make honeymoon reservations for the Turks and Caicos, we have a lot to unpack and some of this luggage is quite heavy.

1

The King and I

> Ultimately, what will make you someone's Queen, is the ability to fit into his Kingdom.

Girlfriend, I know that you feel good! Men are passing you up and clearly, they are blind. You are *wifey* material, a good catch, and a virtuous woman. You know your worth. You are a Queen! You believe, if men would just act right, you could connect with your King. So, what's the issue, what are you missing? What many women forget is, *a Queen is the wife of a King*, that is the historic definition. Ultimately, what will make you someone's Queen, is the ability to fit into his Kingdom.

The King

For the purposes of this book, our references to men, Kings, husbands, potentials, suitors; pertain only to men of quality, substance, standards, spirituality, stability, and high moral character. So often women feel these men don't exist, and inquire, "where are they?" Well, everywhere! Firstly, you need to understand who the King is. Secondly, you must over-stand; he is completely different from the men you have dated in every way. There is a reason you have not attracted the type of quality men you desire. Too many self-proclaimed queens put on the crown prematurely. Before dawning the crown, you must identify the unroyal attributes that are holding you back from palace life. Perhaps you have caught the eye of a King in the past, but couldn't quite attain the crown. To understand how to draw the attention of the King, you must first know who he is.

High Moral Character

The King possesses a high moral character. This does not mean he doesn't have a past, hasn't made mistakes, or is perfect. However, he lives his life by a moral code. He has an honor system. This man's word and his name, are his bond. He is not a free spirit, in other words, he doesn't make up his own rules. The King understands how vital structure and order are and he lives under that banner. The King is a man of faith, and it's his faith, that keeps him grounded.

Financially Stable

The King will never need a place to lay his head, neither would he reach out to anyone in a financial crisis. He handles his business. The King isn't in a financial struggle, he is financially fit in every way, not necessarily *rich*, but financially fit and stable. He has built-up savings, investments, and will likely have property. The King believes in ownership. The King doesn't have foolish spending habits and doesn't concern himself with *keeping up with the Joneses*. The King's family will never need a Go-Fund-Me campaign to bury him, his affairs are in order. The King is also *not* a 50/50 man...

Family Man

The King understands generational wealth is only transferred through the family. The King is going to want children to carry on the legacy and family name, so that future generations will have a foundation. This is quite simply, the reason he works so diligently. It's not just for him, it's for the bloodline. The King won't have unpaid child support. Although people can get into a bind, the King would work at Burger King, before his Queen, or his children would go without. He honors the elders in his family and will bring them into his home in their golden years. He would do the same for his in-laws. He loves all children, and fully understands, they are the future.

Purpose Driven

The King is not looking for his purpose. He is living it. His purpose is never for *just him and his.* This is key. A King denotes, he is over a kingdom, a people, and has an army. He will likely have employees, a team, a tribe, and mentees. If a man does not have mentees, he's not quite a King. Younger men are drawn to successful men, and these people will be around. If you meet a man and he is unsure of his purpose, he is not yet a King. A man of purpose won't be attracted to a woman that's unsure of her own purpose.

Furthermore, he isn't interested in a woman continuing to exert her independence. If she's unwilling to come under the banner of the Kingdom, follow his lead, and build the empire with him, he's simply going to pass her by. **A house divided cannot stand**. Life won't be a fairytale.

Laser Focused

A King is focused, he *does not* have balance, and you should not try to change that. You, however, are supposed to help him in whatever way is needed. This man is the epitome of busy. If you are accustomed to talking and texting with a man all day, forget about trying that with a King. If you constantly disrupt him while he's handling business, you'll be seen as immature and spoiled. He spends most of his time planning, working, executing, and leading. When he gets home, he wants peace, a smile, a warm meal, and a warm bed. If this insults you, then don't date a King.

Leader

If you want to be in more of a partnership, it's no problem. This type of man just won't be for you. There is a reason why companies have one CEO, one President. There is also a reason nearly 70% of all business partnerships fail. Anything with two heads is a monster. When there is no clear leader defined, in any structure, it will lead to mass chaos. Ladies, you understand this concept at work (Company President), sports (Head Coach), places of worship (Senior Pastor), military (General), politics (President), even on cheer squads, there is a Head Cheerleader! When it comes to the family, why is there so much pushback defining a leader?

His Queen

- His Queen must be superior in every way.

- She will be physically attractive to *him*. Not a model, he isn't looking for that.

- She carries herself as a lady, she's classy and always well put together.

- She's a wonderful mother.

- He trusts her, and she supports him fully.

- She's crafted her life into his Kingdom.

- She's all about her family.

- She's a woman of unshakeable faith.

■ She possesses high intelligence and wisdom.

We polled husbands regarding the attributes their wives possessed, that set them apart from other women. One newlywed pollster said, "Men choose the path of least resistance, my wife was peaceful, supportive, and non-combative." Another newlywed pollster said, "I trusted my wife, more than I loved her." High on the list of attributes were God-fearing and compassionate women.

As the Queen, you must be rational, loving, wise, smart, sharp, observant, and hospitable. If you think Kings are choosing popular *social media models,* you are incorrect. Most of those ladies are single. This is a very big misconception, especially among millennials. What a man "likes" and will possibly hang out with, isn't who he marries. In my nearly 25 years in the wedding industry, I can tell you, men, by and large, do not marry *social media models* or the equivalent in my day, *video vixens.* Women who obsess over their outer beauty only, cannot yet relate to the desires of a King. Your mindset is temporal. A King has structure, discipline, order. Qualities you've likely never encountered in men!

The King's life can seem routine, and you must be able to handle not spending a lot of personal time together. Just ask any woman married to a doctor, politician, or high profile man, what it's like. Many women get a false idea that life with a King is full of travel, shopping sprees, and trips to the salon. If you aren't disciplined, bore easily, and need to be entertained, palace life won't work for you at all. Also, consider ladies, there are a lot of women after the King and willing to do anything. While desperation turns him off, her effort will catch his eye. Women today feel the man must do all the work to prove himself. These women are single.

The Queen

Everyone will not connect with the KING, but you will connect with your King. A Queen or a good catch, does not mean you are perfect. It means you are consciously "aware" of who you are and, more importantly, *where* you are in your life.

- Are you working to be the best you that you can possibly be?

- Are you aware of your flaws?

- Do you know your shortcomings and insecurities?

- Are you aware of what pushes your buttons?

- Do you know your weaknesses and triggers?

- What are your toxic traits?

- Are you aware of your masculine energy?

- Do you take the lead?

- Do you often get impatient with men?

- Do you try to get to know who you are dating, his interests, his likes, and dislikes?

Queens-to-be, understand, there are some things about your life that are a total turn-off to a man and you may not be aware of it. Look at this A-Z list of personality types that are King repellant.

A-Z Toxic Personality Traits

- **Analyzing Anita**. Anita obsesses over every little detail and thing her man says and does. She is constantly scouring his social media page for new activities and thoroughly researches every woman that makes a comment. Anita takes everything to heart. She calls her girlfriends all day, constantly asking what they think "this" or "that" means. Anita rarely lets her man know that she is overanalyzing their every conversation and interaction, but he feels it, nonetheless.

- **Bad Vibes Bernice.** Bernice is impossible to deal with. Her attitude and vibe are just horrid. Bernice has a sharp tongue and is rude and nasty to everyone around her. Bernice offends very easily and feels that people are always attacking her. She is just downright mean and unpleasant. Bernice has no problem attracting passive-aggressive males, a King would never look her way.

- **Complaining Chrissy.** Chrissy complains about her job, family, friends, flat tires, bills, and posts on social media. Complaining Chrissy sees something wrong with everything, except her own actions. She also does not look at the glass as half full, but half empty. If she goes out to dinner, it's guaranteed, she will complain about the food and send it back several times. Chrissy, you can be sure; this attitude will quickly seem very unroyal to a King.

- **Doing too much Donna.** Girl, just stop! You are doing way too much. You don't let the man breathe. You don't allow him to call or text you first. You must comment on every one of his posts. You send him selfies all day. You post subliminal messages online. You plan all the dates. You tell him way too much of your personal business way too soon. Girlfriend, you are doing too much to attract a King!

- **Evil Erica.** Erica is downright vengeful, spiteful, and hateful. Erica is the woman that uses her children as pawns if she wants to get even with their father. Erica has no good thing in her. She will destroy homes, careers, and families. She always initially comes like an angel in disguise but leaves a trail of destruction behind her.

■ **Fake Feather.** Feather is faker than a $3 bill. Feather pretends she is everyone's friend while secretly sowing discord among her group. Feather throws rocks then hides her hand. Feather will smile in your face while watching someone put a dagger in your back. A King can't trust Feather with the serious affairs of the Kingdom.

■ **Guarded Gina.** Gina is more guarded than the crowned Jewels at the British Museum. Gina is tired of opening her heart, only to be let down, time and time again. She has placed a big sign on her forehead reading "Closed Until Further Notice". She's over it all and happy with her rigid schedule, frequent spa dates, and new cat. Gina is locked out and she refuses to let anyone in.

■ **Heavenly Hannah**. Jesus is her Valentine, and she has a life of prayer, fasting, celibacy, and church. Hannah will break out her pocket bible and begin a full altar call in the middle of a dinner date. Hannah was taught that godly men will find that type of "saintly" persona attractive. These overzealous church sisters aren't masculine nor feminine, they are over spiritual. Slow down Hannah, it's okay to talk about subjects other than, the church bake sale!

■ **Isolated Ilene.** Ilene, love. A King can't find you sitting in the house with the blinds drawn all day! Ilene is very anti-social, yet she inwardly longs to get out and be around people and even meet a man. Ilene is extremely shy and unsure of herself, she's awkward and doesn't quite fit in. With some guidance and direction, Ilene could be ready to connect with a good man.

- **Jokester Joy.** Joy is bubbly, fun, and is always the life of the party. However, life is not just a party, Joy! Her imbalance has hindered Joy from becoming a fully functional adult. She's spoiled by her parents and is extremely immature. Joy still has some growing up to do. The King requires a grown woman that can balance playtime but knows when playtime is over.

- **Kind Kelly.** Kelly is a nice, humble, and kind woman, too kind in fact. Kelly lacks a keen sense of discernment and often allows people to run over her. Kelly gives people the benefit of the doubt all too often. Although this will give many men an opportunity to swoop in and save her, a King may view her ability to not put herself before others, as a rather low-value trait. Kelly, be kind to yourself first and others will follow suit.

- **Lying Lina.** We are not even sure if Lina is her name! Lina is just one big liar. She lies about things she doesn't even need to lie about. She makes up stories to appear to be bigger in life than what she really is. She will lie cheat, even steal. Lying Lina can't be trusted, and she can't enter even into the vicinity of the Kingdom.

- **Money Hungry Mona.** Mona doesn't chase dreams, she chases dollars. The only value she sees in a man is what his money can buy her. If he's not spending wads of cash on her, she's spending no time with him. Mona has mastered the art of manipulating men for money and has no conscience about it. Many men may be fooled by Mona's looks, but her motives will be crystal clear in a short amount of time.

- **Narcissistic Nina.** Nina is the worst type of woman. Nina plays mind manipulation games with people to get what she wants. If she feels someone is not with her program, Nina begins to use their weaknesses against them. She can slowly break a person down to the least common denominator, leaving her victims psychologically damaged for years. The dangerous part about Nina is, she can make her way into the palace, Kings should be aware of Nina.

■ **One Track Olivia.** If your conversation consists of the latest celebrity scoop, or reality show reunion run down, you can forget about being with a King. Kings seek deep, mature, and stimulating conversation, they thrive on it. While you do not need to know the details of the Revolutionary War, being well-rounded is a necessary stimulant to a quality suitor.

■ **Ph.D. Patricia.** Dr. Pat is a walking, talking resume. Her entire existence is her educational and professional accomplishments. She won't settle for a man beneath her academic and professional level. What she's missing is, the King doesn't choose for those reasons alone. Pat is aggressive, unyielding, and uncompromising. All things completely unfeminine and unattractive to a King.

■ **Queen B.** Queen B has already crowned herself and is just waiting on the chariot to whisk her away. Queen B is ready, so she thinks. No matter what Queen B does, good, bad, or indifferent, she believes herself appointed title, gives her access to the finer things in life. Queen B doesn't understand, she's not entitled to the crown, but her attitude of entitlement tells her otherwise.

■ **Rumor Mill Renee.** Renee is obsessed with life. Someone else's life! Renee is the person people go-to for the latest rumor and gossip, and she doesn't mind spreading the rumors either. She can't keep a secret to save her life and doesn't mind "spilling the tea" to social media. One of the keys to a man's heart is being able to hold his private business and secrets in confidence. Renee doesn't have those keys on her ring.

- **Self-Conscious**. Sheila, just don't date, period. It will end in disaster. Quite simply if you do not love yourself, where you are right now, don't expect anyone else to. This is not to say you aren't working on areas in your life that need improvement. It means you accept and love who you are and the journey. There is no faking this, so don't even try. Get healing and prayer before venturing out on the dating market again.

- **Thirsty Tanya.** Desperation to a man signals you are not a Queen; you are not royalty. No man wants a woman that no other man is after! Your desperation shows him you have no other options, and this is a sure-fire way to attract predators and repel Kings.

- **Unstable Uma.** Uma's life is unstable due to a pattern of irresponsible decisions. She constantly moves from place to place because she lives above her means. Jumps from job to job because she just quits on impulse with no plan in place. Uma doesn't have what it takes to go it long term with a man, or even friends. An unstable lifestyle will be sure to keep you on the outer courts of the castle.

- **Vain Vicky.** Vicky thinks she's already in the palace. Vicky believes her looks, pedigree, and family background puts her head and shoulders above everyone else. She believes men are lucky that she would even give them a second look, much less a date. Vicky isn't worried about being picked by a King, it's in her blood to do so. Vicky has naturally what many women pay thousands of dollars for, but her rotten aristocratic privileged attitude, won't get her far. A King craves a woman who is humble yet confident, not puffed up and vain.

- **Wild Wendy.** Wendy thinks it's okay to twerk in public and have inappropriate pictures on social media. Wendy gets into arguments often and still talks about physically fighting. Wendy gets sloppy drunk and high. Wendy's sex life is completely wild. She feels she can live her life the way she wants with no judgment. She is loud, lewd, crude, and defends wearing bonnets and house slippers in public. Sweetheart, you'll be lucky if you could date the palace beggar.

- **Xerotic Xena.** Xerotic characterizes an "extra dry" condition. And that's Xena. She's dry, lackluster, unenthused, and nothing excites her. There is nothing worse than planning a special day for someone, only for the recipient to give a dry response. She's a bore, has no conversational skills, and lacks the energy needed to stimulate a real man.

- **Zany Zoey.** Zoey is absolutely bat #### crazy! She will break the windows out of her man's car if she suspects he is cheating. Zoey will go to her man's job and confront his work wife. Zoey will stake out her man's home and follow him. This nut case is very controlling and insists her guy acts in a way she desires, or he will have hell to pay. Zoey is Zany but she can be dangerous, Kings should stay far away!

Admitting

Were you able to see yourself in any of these toxic personality types? If not, give this list to a friend, and see if they have a differing opinion. You may be shocked at their feedback! While this list covered quite a few "man repellant" personality types, there are dozens more. It is vitally important that you, know thy self! Appearing perfect and not recognizing that you have flaws, *is a flaw.* If you become ill and require emergency room treatment, you first must go through Admitting. In the Admitting Room, necessary information is gathered for the best treatment. If you don't know your symptoms, how can you get the proper care?

No man expects you to be perfect. Men appreciate women that try to better their own lives. When a man sees you are actively working to improve your own life, he knows you will do the same for him. Beyond your personality flaws, there are some major areas in life that you should be handling now. These areas should be handled whether you desire to date at this time or not. As mature adults, we must have our lives in order. Trust me, a King will give pause to a woman whose "house" seems to be unreasonably out of order.

Set Your House in Order

Finances

Are you stable enough financially, that you won't go into a relationship being overly needy? If your bank accounts are in overdraft, credit cards maxed, and car payments behind, you may choose a man simply because he can take care of those bills. Girlfriend, you know we have all fallen victim, or at least been tempted, by a sugar daddy! However, to a King, you appear to be one big pile of debt. A pile of debt he will have to pay down.

Health

Are you dealing with a major health crisis that may hinder your relationships or potentials? Are you thriving to be in the best physical shape you can be? Do you attempt to eat healthy, exercise, and take care of your temple? Especially in today's health-conscious climate, many Kings are putting their health in high priority, and they will look for their mate to do the same.

Family

Do you have family issues or struggles that may prevent you from dating? Perhaps your family situation is at the crisis stage, and it's not a good idea to start something new. Maybe your children are young and need more of your time. Maybe you are taking care of a sick or aging relative. Perchance you have concerns about being infertile. These are all major issues that will affect your romantic life.

Career

Are you totally focused on your career right now? Do you travel a lot and really don't have time to date? Do you have a heavy caseload in school? Is your schedule totally hectic? Let me tell you, ladies. I don't care how busy a man is; he wants to see his lady as much as he can. Double standard? Yes, but it's so true. This doesn't mean a career-driven woman can't find a companion who is understandable, but this could be a major source of stress for a new relationship.

Baggage

Are you going through a divorce? I'll say this loud and clear: Please do not date anyone until divorce papers have been signed, sealed, and delivered! This causes nothing but undue stress. If you are still dealing with a bad breakup or heartbreak, have parenting issues with your children's father, or perhaps you have legal or criminal cases pending, these are major issues. I'd advise you to work on unpacking your luggage before taking another trip.

> Understand, becoming a Queen, is not about being perfect. It's about understanding, accepting, and loving who you are, right now. Pretending as though your life is perfect, is a sign that you are not comfortable with your life. If you aren't comfortable with yourself, neither will a King be comfortable bringing you into his palace.

2

The Dating Market

Ladies, you can't connect with a man sitting at home, watching
Lifetime reruns, and eating bonbons!

Boy, oh boy! The Dating Market! And a market it is! There is plenty of meat, frozen foods, canned vegetables, and a good variety of mixed nuts! Let's not forget the GMOs! Appears to be the real thing, even taste like the real thing, but it's not! The first thing you need to know about the dating market, as a single woman, is what you see most of the time is not what you get. Not trying to scare you, but I'm trying to prepare you, especially if you don't date a lot. There are a lot of predators looking for prey. In the dating market, you have men looking for sex, a jump-off, a good time, and nothing serious. You have little boys looking for a sugar mama to pay his bills, men adding women to their growing roster, and some that just don't know what in the world they want.

There are also plenty of quality men that are looking to marry. These men are out there, but you need to first know where to find them and what they are looking for. A man of quality is not looking for a good woman; he is looking for the best woman for *him*. Not a foreign concept ladies! How many good men have you met, that are not good for *you?*

In the dating market, women often run down a list of their career accomplishments when trying to prove they are a good catch. And while education, academic achievements, and drive are very important to a quality man, he is looking for something more. Your accomplishments are just that, your accomplishments. A man needs to know that you will respect him, and you will have his back through thick and thin. Are you a soft place to lay his head at the end of the day? Do you admire him, and will you let him lead you? I'm not suggesting that you downplay your achievements. I certainly wouldn't do that for my own. Ladies, overstand this, your resume does not weigh as heavy on the scales for a man, as you would think.

In the dating market, it's important to know where to go meet new people. The short answer is, everywhere! Every place you go, at every minute of the day, you could meet the love of your life. My cousin met her future husband in the parking lot of her bank, she was standing in line, and he noticed her!

- **Feel and look your bes**t, everywhere you go. Now, that does not mean you have on *full* smoky eye and five-inch Jimmy Choos. It means if you have on leggings and a t-shirt, you rock them!

- **Smile, ladies!** A woman's smile does something to a man. Make eye contact. Stop being scared! Let men know that it's okay to approach you.

- **Start a conversation**. You never have to ask a man out on a date; just put yourself in a position to be asked. While shopping in the dating market, you must be open and friendly. A man needs to know that you are approachable.

Places to Meet Quality Men

Grocery Store

I find that single men today, not only cook but cook well! So, it's very easy to strike up a conversation while picking up a bottle of balsamic vinaigrette.

Fitness Clubs

While I don't personally like to run into a hot guy while I am sweaty, this is a really great place to meet men that you see on a regular basis. Just start a conversation, ladies! Ask him about equipment. You know, be a girl!

Bookstores/Coffeeshops

Businessmen, intellectuals, visionaries, students, and all kinds of great guys spend hours at bookstores and coffee shops. They will be studying, writing, and having meetings. This is another great way to strike up a conversation.

Sporting Events

Ladies, if you know someone hosting a co-ed sports event or tailgating party, please go! Men will be there!

Social Events

Networking, weddings, holiday parties, fundraisers, religious and business seminars are other great ways to meet good men who are forward-thinking with goals.

Classes

Enrolling in a class, whether on campus or just to learn a special skill, is a good way to interact and ask questions of eligible bachelors.

Now that you know where to go, it's important that you get out and explore. Ladies, you can't connect with a man sitting at home, watching Lifetime reruns, and eating bonbons! In your exploration of the market, be conscious, there are a variety of rotten meats and expired milk cartons. Don't let unhealthy foods wrapped in attractive packaging, tempt you. Organic selections are available. For better quality, you may have to drive a little further and change the market where you typically shop. Take time to read the ingredients on the labels, and for goodness' sake, don't rush and grab the sale items near the checkout!

3

Swipe Left

> "A staggering one in six marriages are formed through online dating!"

It's a jungle in the world of online dating. Just twenty years ago, you had to get out of the house to meet people. Dating now is downloading an app and "swiping left" until you find a profile that intrigues you. It's scary. People are scary and, for the most part, it's a bunch of married men hiding behind fake profiles, lying about everything from their income to their age, their weight, and height (apparently many men don't know what "athletic build" is). Yes, that part is true. So, why even bother? Well, here are a few reasons:

1. The Internet is how we run our lives now. We pay bills, bank, work, attend class, socialize, and network online. You probably found out about this book online! It's quite natural that now most people are dating online.
2. It's no longer taboo; it's the norm. It doesn't make you look desperate and lonely. Yes, you are putting yourself out there. But that's the whole point of dating, right?

The key to online dating is properly educating yourself and having your eyes wide open. The promises, sweet nothings, and knights in shining armor, will have the wisest of women fooled! Don't believe everything you read. For the most part, you are not special to your online *boo thing*. The same guy that messaged you just messaged twenty other girls with the same manufactured copy-and-pasted message. He just got excited because you responded.

There are so many dating apps and websites, it's hard to navigate which one to explore. The top dating apps are Grindr, Meetme, Match.com, PlentyofFish, Hinge, OkCupid, Tinder (Zuckerman, 2020). In the online world, the dating ratio is **39% men to 25% women** (Online Dating Report, 2017). Your chances online to meet a man, go up tremendously!

Let's start off with some great news, a bit later, we will go over the not-so-great news.

Positive Online Dating Statistics

- One in five relationships got their start through online dating. (Zuckerman, 2020)
- A staggering one in six marriages are formed through online dating! (Zuckerman, 2020)
- 39% of online dating app users went on dates with people they have met. (Zuckerman, 2020)
- 12% of Americans that are married or in committed relationships, met their mates through dating apps. (Matthews, n.d.)
- People who meet online get married quicker than people who connect traditionally. (Matthews, n.d.)
- Business owners make up (11%) of the online dating population globally. (Online Dating Report, 2017)
- eHarmony's divorce rate is 3.86%! This is lower than the US 50% rate of divorce. Astounding! (Matthews, n.d.)

Hope that made you feel a bit more positive about online dating!

Her Profile

To start your online dating journey, overstand, your online image is absolutely everything. Your online profile, just like your resume, says a lot about you and what you will attract. I don't care how creative your wording is, all women will eventually meet a liar, loser, or leech. You can dramatically increase your chances of a good catch by portraying the right image.

- **Please, please, please use current pictures!** Please do not pretend to be someone you are not, and please don't alter your image. The last thing you want is to finally meet a man in person and you are not who you said you were online. Your feelings will be beyond hurt! So, keep your photos at least six months current. Have several headshots of you smiling, and please have a few full-body shots. I don't care how awkward you feel about your body. Men are visual and they must see the whole you. Please ladies, ease off the provocative, bent-over in the club, "Hot Girl Summer" poses unless you are trying to attract that type of guy. We can be sexy and sassy without being trashy! Have at least six to eight current photos and at least two or three full-body photos. In most of them, you should be smiling.

- **Don't lie!** State your correct age, height, and your career. Please don't say that you have a degree, and you don't. Ladies don't lie about your weight description! Girlfriend, you know you have more than a "few extra pounds" on you. Many men meet women from dating apps, that often manipulate pictures to appear 100-150 pounds, less than what they are! Do not do this ladies! Trust my two-plus decades in the wedding business, brides come in all shapes and sizes, including pear and Sponge Bob, so no need to deceive!

- **Your profile name** should be cute and unique. Err on the side of fun and catchy, not too serious, too spiritual, or too sleazy sounding. "Cutieinthecity" or "Detroitgirlsrock" can work. However, "Dezgettingpaper" or "BrendawaitingonBoaz" cannot!

- **About Me section**. Please know that most guys don't have time to read six paragraphs on your profile. So please keep it as short and sweet as possible. Make it about you and what you bring to the table, and a little bit of what you are looking for in a mate. Stay positive. Please don't post "no games" in your About Me section. Don't talk about your dog, cat, or even your kids too much. Talk about you. They need to know you. Also, don't sound too desperate or look like an ad for an escort service. Let men know you have standards, just don't sound too rigid. A quality man is not looking for an angry or direct woman. He is looking for someone light-hearted and easy-going. His life is stressful enough.

- **Your Ideal Mate section**. Here, you can state everything from a certain ethnicity, height, body type, geographic location, education, and many other factors. I will say this, ladies! Be open! If your profile says you prefer someone who is six feet, with a six-pack and making six figures, chances are, you may be passing up a great 5'10" guy making 60K with a little belly flab! Focus more on his inner qualities. The good man you seek is sometimes hiding behind a package you didn't expect. So, just be at least open to dating someone you wouldn't normally date!

Now that your profile is live, please expect contact from anybody and everybody under the sun. Please remember, most are fakers and looking for sex. Block and continue! Don't let a few frogs deter you. But still, be open to meeting some good men and even new friends. Here are some causes to pause when online dating:

His Profile

- **No pictures or old, outdated pictures.** In this day of technology, we know recent pictures when we see them. Just like you, he should have a variety of updated pics that show his entire body and a close-up of his face. You should be able to tell if the pics are old or not! If he only has two or three pics, be very careful!

- **Vague profile and vague messages.** Use caution with the "Hey, what's up?" and "Hey beautiful!" A man that doesn't take the time to properly introduce himself should not garner a response. Beware of general messages. A man that is serious will quote something from your profile like, "Oh, you like salsa dancing, too?" That shows he at least took the time to read.

- **No information** in his profile. Keep it moving like a freight train!

- **Love Bombing.** If he's saying, "You are the one," "You are what I've been looking for," or he says, "You seem like a woman I could marry," cause for pause! Men like this know what you want to hear, and for the most part, it works.

- **Slow!** Now I understand getting to know someone takes time. Beware of men that are slow to respond and slower to take the conversation from the Internet to the phone, and then in person.

- **Flaky.** If he breaks, changes, and cancels plans often, he is someone that may have something to hide.

Never meet anyone without having a few phone conversations. Be sure to have a video chat. That way, you all see each other and know if there is mutual interest. Never prolong the meeting process. I can't stress this enough. Meet face-to-face quickly. For some, this is a day. For others, it's a week or two. Honestly, if the conversation goes past a month, that is a red flag (stop). Allowing a man to be in your personal space without a meeting, essentially means, you've accepted a non-physical relationship with a stranger. This speaks a lot about you, don't allow it. Remember meeting online is essentially a blind date. But it doesn't have to be! With video chat, phone conversation, etc., it should not have to be a guessing game.

Safety

We cannot talk about online dating without talking about safety. Practice these safety tips when you first meet someone, not just online, but in general:

1. DO NOT EVER give out your address, your place of employment, or places you frequent, such as your place of worship or gym.

2. Get a vanity phone number from Google Voice as opposed to using your cell number. Someone can find your address just by using your phone number. It's free, and I'd highly suggest it.

3. NEVER allow them to pick you up. Drive your car and let him drive his car. If he needs you to pick him up, that's a date that you don't need to go on.

Social Media Dating

Beyond online dating sites, many people connect and meet via social media sites, especially Facebook (that was its original function). Facebook, to me, is a bit better than online dating, although there could be some potential "Catfishers" (fake profiles). In general, you get a better sense of who the person is through their posts, pictures, and interactions with others. It's a bonus if you all have friends in common. But of course, take the same precautions as you would with online dating.

Out of State

- I caution against meeting someone out of the country. I know a few people that did it and it worked out, but that is a huge game of Russian roulette. So be sure you want to play it. If you happen to hit it off with someone out of state, there is a whole lot to consider:

- Please video chat, and video chat often. The last thing you want is to take a trip and neither one of you are feeling one another. Don't do it!

- Other than the issue of distance, you really want to follow the same guidelines as you do with online dating. The kicker comes in when it's time to meet in person.

Now, depending on how far you all are a part, it could be as simple as a few hours in a car ride. But then, of course, the distance could be coastal where someone must get on a plane. Ladies, I highly suggest that you allow the man to come to see you. That means he will arrange his own transportation and lodging. You should not offer for him to stay at your place at this first meeting. I don't care how long you have been talking, video chatting, or how well you think you know him. You really don't.

If for some reason, his schedule does not allow him to come to you, it is proper for him to arrange your transportation in his hometown. Never fly to a place where neither of you knows anyone. For the sake of safety, I highly suggest no one has access to where you are sleeping or staying. I would suggest getting your own lodging and ground transportation. Of course, there are exceptions to the rules, and you must always use practical wisdom. But please, do not drop your guard before you even meet!

Is this being overly cautious? Maybe a bit, but there are just too many stories that don't turn out well. It's better to protect yourself than go in blind. I am not saying don't take a chance, throw caution to the wind, and enjoy your life. I'm just saying, be careful. When dating out of state, do not get serious about the relationship until you visit his home to meet his family and friends and vice versa. That advice applies to any relationship! It's quite easy for someone to carry on another life when you only meet in hotels.

Adverse Online Dating Statistics

1. 45% of online dating users in the U.S. feel frustrated by the process. (Online Dating Report, 2017)

2. 38% are finding difficulty connecting with people desiring the same kind of relationship.(Online Dating Report, 2017)

3. 61% of men claim they do not get enough messages from women there are interested in. (Online Dating Report, 2017)

4. Women, on the other hand, are five times more likely to receive too many messages. (Online Dating Report, 2017)

Adverse Mental Health Effects

Online dating comes with an extremely unique set of possible damaging effects, especially for those who may be dealing with untreated mental and traumatic issues. Some of the adverse effects of online dating may shock you.

1. Spending more time on the dating app than you should. Relationship Coach, Eddie Fernandez, suggests "No more than three times a week, 20 minutes a day maximum. Longer times could begin to affect your actual physical health, outlook on life and social life." (Hernandez, 2021)

2. Online dating apps should not replace meeting people tradition-ally in your everyday routine, school, work, social activities, spe-cial events, etc. (Hernandez, 2021)

3. As discussed earlier, a very real danger of online dating, espe-cially for those that may be like a deer in headlights, is emotional attachment. Flattery, and constant communication, sometimes for years, without a meeting, is dangerous territory. You can be *love-bombed,* only to find out, your crush is a married man, with a wife, and five children. It bears repeating, do not allow things to go over a few weeks without meeting in person.

4. Portraying someone online that you aren't in real life. Either by a fake profile or a made-up persona.(Hernandez, 2021). Women may play the bad girl online engaging in bad behavior they would never act out in real life. This may seem like harmless fun, but it is not.

5. If you are the only or main one starting conversations and meet-up dates are constantly canceled or postponed, cut them off im-mediately. (Hernandez, 2021)

Trust your gut. If it doesn't feel right, it probably isn't. If he texts you all the time, but won't call you, he is probably married. If his life is a mystery and you really don't know anything about him, it's because he is probably hiding something. Do the right thing for yourself and move on; but please do not close the door to on-line or out-of-state dating. In fact, in my private Facebook group, three couples that met and married lived out of state!

4

Fatal Attraction

"Just like a dope fiend, there is something about that experience, although damaging in the end, that you just can't get enough of."

Do you enter relationships, situation-ships, or confuse-a-ships with the same type of men repeatedly, with absolutely near-fatal, toxic, and damaging results? What is it in you, that keeps attracting them, and why do you keep allowing it? Is there a reason why some women always find themselves involved with married men, cheaters, losers, narcissists, and mamas' boys? Could it be that these men sense something in these women? Absolutely. However, sometimes it's not the man at all, it's you.

The Ride

Do you attract the non-committal man? The man that is emotionally unavailable? The narcissist? In the beginning, things go super-fast. You have an amazing time and can't get enough of each other. You text all day, call all day and then CRASH. I need to give you a very hard pill to swallow ladies, so get a cup of water ready. What you are feeling is excitement and a surge of adrenaline, like an exciting roller coaster **RIDE**. You are not getting to know this person. you don't love them; you are having superficial **experiences**.

While on a coaster, you are only feeling a rush, there is no time to really observe who is sharing the seat with you. You do not love them. You love the experience of them. If I could get women to stop concentrating on how much money a man spends on a date, we could get somewhere. Why? Lavish and exciting dates don't get you closer to knowing who a man really is. It actually blinds you to who he is. In the grand scheme of getting to know someone, a nice walk in the park will do wonders.

Initially, you are thrilled to be having this experience with this man. But after the ride stops, the *red flags* begin blaring in the wind. Now, this once exciting ride is filled with inconsistencies, broken promises, confusion, and a lack of effort. But you stayed. Understand, you only stayed remembering the ride. Hoping to capture that feeling again.

There is one way to fix this pattern, SLOW DOWN! **Narcissists especially, reel you in with experiences and get you addicted to the ride.** If you take your time and walk through the park, instead of jumping in line for the *demon drop*, you may realize, this is a man you don't want to sit next to at all.

Fantasy Island

Ladies, often our attraction is what we perceive the man has to offer. It's not actually him, what's inside of him and what makes him tick as a person. These near-fatal attractions always start off lightning-fast, and after the impending "crash," begins a series of arguments. You are frustrated because your fantasy, has now become your nightmare. This man is not who you envisioned.

My ladies, sometimes the adrenaline is so high, you stay with a man, you don't really care for (although you have convinced yourself you do). It's like you are an addict, needing a fix. This is not settling, this is fantasizing. You will stay in this relationship for years, remembering the exhilarating journey in the beginning. You stay in constant conflict with the man because he hasn't been able to recapture the experience. That's not love, that's fantasy and strong delusion. Just like a dope fiend, you keep going back for more, knowing full well it will end with a fiery crash.

Self-Sabotage

Deeper still, some women deep down are not prepared and are downright scared of marriage and deeper commitments. So much so, they self-sabotage anything that may be real. It takes a lot of deep introspection to realize this. Taking a high-speed dating ride, in the beginning, is not reflective of real life. It's not reflective of your responsibilities and daily routine as a couple. When these women realize the ride is over and must return to the real world, they self-destruct. The man in this instance didn't do anything at all. The woman was just downright afraid and ill-prepared for the commitment. Commitment is not an everlasting date. Marriage and real relationships are work. Self-sabotage is prevalent today because so many women were raised without examples of real relationships and marriage. So, the television image of Cinderella being whisked away to the palace is the foundation of their love lives.

Serial Dating

Ladies, do you jump out of one relationship to another, with little to no time in between? Do you realize this may be more damaging than you think? Side note: some experts believe serial dating, in and of itself may not be harmful (Ferguson, 2021). However, if you are on a merry-go-round, of going- nowhere relationships, you may need to stop the ride and get off the horse. A few signs you are a serial dater or serial monogamist are:

- Being single, leaves you feeling lonely, and you suffer from self-esteem issues.(Ferguson, 2021)
- You won't leave a relationship until another one is lined up.(Ferguson, 2021)
- You easily bore and become restless in relationships. (Ferguson, 2021)
- As soon as one relationship ends, you waste no time getting into another.(Ferguson, 2021)
- Your relationships typically get very intense, very early on. (Ferguson, 2021)

I need to address boredom in relationships, and this may sting. Many women use this as a bragging right. Some ladies think swapping partners when she bores of them, makes her exciting. The underlying message is; men must constantly keep her entertained to stay in her presence. Not actually. It is fear of commitment. Once the excitement dies down and she faces the reality of a relationship, she will self-destruct. Being constantly bored is a sign of immaturity and shows you aren't mentally or emotionally stable enough to be in a relationship. You have the mind of a child, like Jokester Joy in Chapter One. Real-life is not a party, it has responsibilities, duties, and darn right hard work. Stop using the excuse of boredom to mask your fear of commitment.

If you recognize serial dating has become an issue for you, answer these questions:

- What relationships did you see as examples growing up? (Ferguson, 2021)
- Do you think being single will reflect badly on you? (Ferguson, 2021)
- How do you think about your loved ones and acquaintances who are single? (Ferguson, 2021)
- How do you handle loneliness? (Ferguson, 2021)

To finally connect with the right man for you, get off the serial dating Ferris wheel and change your behavior. Stop allowing countless people to have access to your life. Reserve that space in your life ONLY for the man that will love, care and appreciate you.

Unhealed Trauma

Staying with a man that mistreats you, strings you along, devalues or disrespects you, reflects what you think about yourself. And he knows it! There is something in us saying, "This situation and this person is not right." Yet, because we share good times in between the bad, we justify staying with this person. We make excuses for bad behavior. If your toddler told you their babysitter was mistreating them, would you keep taking them back? I hope not. So why do you keep allowing your heart to be abused? I hope that you will recognize this and make the necessary steps toward healing. Some of you want companionship so bad, you ignore the sirens, bells, and whistles going off loudly in your ears. One bell we never hear though is the bell inside of us.

Childhood Trauma

Children who experience a childhood traumatic event may have a lifetime of healing ahead of them. According to treamentspecialist.com, this stems from the development of the brain which impacts the child's ability to understand or process the traumatic event. Causes of childhood trauma may include:

- Sexual abuse
- Physical abuse
- Domestic abuse
- Natural disasters
- Serious car accident
- The sudden death of a loved one
- Serious medical illness or injury

- Kidnapping
- Experiencing school violence

The child's underdeveloped brain produces fear-related hormones, such as cortisol, which can become a survival mechanism. This affects adulthood behaviors and patterns. If the trauma or abuse was repeated and not a single occurrence, this further worsens the condition (Symptoms of Childhood Trauma in Adults, 2019). Seeking a combination of professional, spiritual, and familial support is vital to move forward from childhood traumas.

Self-Reflection

Ladies, many of you don't realize you have also hurt and damaged men that invested time, love, and finances in you. This is huge. Sometimes we have forgotten the broken hearts we have left along the way. Some of you reading this have cheated on spouses, lied about paternity, and even mistreated men that loved you. I will say, if the person is still alive, at least apologize. This isn't about reconciliation; this is about stopping a pattern of behavior. You can't expect a new love in your life with unfinished business in your past.

> The bottom line, you cannot value a man or anyone else, until you learn to value yourself. Decide what you want and deserve. Learn your bad habits and root causes of those issues and take time to heal. Until you do all of that, you are doomed to repeat damaging behaviors that result in near-fatal consequences.

5

Value Systems

> "If you are in debt, have horrible credit and little to no savings, you start looking like an added expense to a man, rather than an asset."

Can I be honest, some of the things we "value" in a man, are down-right superficial, immature, and lack substance. I know women who have passed up very good men for trivial reasons. The word "settling" is so overused, it's lost meaning. Who told you, that settling for a grounded, mature, and responsible man, with a solid set of values, was beneath you? This attitude will keep you on Ms. Independent Island indefinitely. It's time to re-evaluate the things we hold dear to our "list" of values.

Education

I was having a conversation with a professional gentleman that held a bachelor's degree in Finance. A woman he was dating with a Ph.D. in Education, had just broken things off with him. Her reasoning: and I quote, "I need a man that is on my level, not someone that will bring me down." My sisters! I understand, appreciate, and applaud your educational accomplishments, they are to be commended and respected. However, rejecting a man **solely** on his level of degree, borderlines on insanity. Stop the madness!

Instead of judging him by his degrees, listen to him. Is he knowledge-able in areas, well-versed, well-spoken? Is he driven? Is he successful at what he does? Is he financially stable? What are his interests, hobbies, community involvement, spiritual life, and family values? What do you all have in common? Dismissing a man, strictly because his de-grees don't line the wall as high as yours, can potentially cut you off from the love of your life.

Physical Attraction vs. Chemistry

Girlfriend, do you think men are shallow when it comes to physical attraction? In my observation, women can be just as shallow, if not more! Oh, yes, ladies! It's time to own it. But what is the attraction? There are tons of attractive men everywhere. Now, what is attractive to you may be hideous, not-in-this-lifetime-nor-the-next to another sister. But most of us need to admit that we have somewhat of a type.

A fitness trainer may insist on dating a man who is in peak physical form. Due to her lifestyle, that is not a ridiculous request. To the fitness trainer I say, a little belly flab can be worked out, while a nasty attitude cannot. Quite often, we are so caught up in a person's looks, we over-look their character. I am not saying that you must kiss a frog, but a man's looks, just like a woman's, can fade over time. What if a hand-some person today falls ill and looks unattractive tomorrow? Will you love him any less? I'm not saying physical attraction is not important, however, you have dated men all your life that you were physically at-tracted to, and where exactly did that lead you?

You will be physically attracted to many men during your dating life, but *chemistry* is something that is electric. That amazing connection that most of us only get with a handful of people. Chemistry is mag-netic. When you have chemistry with a person, it lasts. Attraction fades. Ladies, what you want in a future mate is chemistry. If you have it with someone, cherish it because it doesn't happen often. Do not confuse chemistry with lust, they are not the same. When you have chemistry with someone, conversations are effortless, and your connections are not forced but very organic.

Faith

This can be tricky; I personally know many couples with differing religious beliefs, who love each other and make their relationship work. On the flip side, I've seen couples that attend the same house of worship and end up in divorce court time after time. I address this in my play "Unequally Yoked." Can love really conquer all, even with spiritual differences?

Faith and belief systems are very serious relationship factors. Some women are open to men with differing religious views, others would never date a man that doesn't share her faith. A man that is firmly rooted in faith, religion, or spiritual practice, for the most part, is seeking a woman who holds those same beliefs. Most religions call for a certain amount of discipline, honor, and for their practitioners to live by a moral code. This begs the question; if a woman is rooted in her faith, why would she marry a man, that is not? If your belief system is strong and intact, this should be an area you won't compromise.

Family Values

Family values are often overlooked and downplayed in the dating process, and they never should be. A person's value system makes them who they are or in some cases, who they are not. Are you a person that is strongly connected to the family? Well, sister, a man that doesn't value family, may want to put your elderly father in a nursing home, when you wanted to care for him in your home. You are ultimately putting a man at the head of your family who does not value family. How will this work?

It's very important that you know the way he was raised. Were his parents married, divorced or was he raised in a single-parent home? Was he adopted, raised in a foster home, or lived with other relatives? How is his relationship with his parents, siblings? Did he know his grandparents, was he raised with an "It takes a village mentality" or a "me against the world" mindset? If he was previously married or has children, what is his relationship like with them or his previous exes? If you are dating for marriage, these things are key. They are also key for yourself.

If you were a woman raised in an environment that was not conducive to family, chances are your outlook is totally different. Surprisingly, many men refuse to date women who were not raised with a father in their lives. Why? We actually polled men on this. They claim these women typically don't know the function, purpose, or value of a man beside his wallet. They don't understand the protective nature of a man and the value he brings to a family. Mainly, women without fathers in their lives, don't know how to let a man lead.

Materialism

Much of today's world is about material gain and possessions. Financial stability and materialism are vastly different. In many instances, women will value materialism and put pressure on their mates to provide these things for them. One example is, purchasing a $150,000 home the family can afford or going into debt for a $350,000 home that will put a major strain on the household budget. It's the "Keeping up with the Joneses" mindset. You must lease the latest car, travel to the most exotic places, and have the flashiest jewelry, no matter what suffers in the home. Materialism can literally destroy your life. Being practical and sensible does not happen for people who are materialistic in nature. They value materials and substances over quality.

Integrity

People with integrity find wallets with identification and return them to the owners. People with integrity don't intentionally deceive or take advantage of others. Persons with integrity do their best, to be honest on taxes and heavens forbid, they would never fabricate data to get a PPP loan! Now, let me be clear, no human on earth is 100% honest. We can all admit a time or two we bent or broke the rules. However, if scheming is your livelihood, if you have no problem lying to get what you want, this is a major break in a person's value system that should not be overlooked. Ladies, you may be that person, if not, you should never accept this type of person as a mate. A person of integrity values their name and character above all else.

Finances

The outlook on finances is truly one of the most critical in any relationship. Before connecting with a man, what do you expect? Are you expecting the man to carry the full weight of the bills in the traditional sense? Are you open to splitting the financial load? This is very important. Many men hold the belief, that the man should be responsible as the head of the home. However, in exchange, you need to know what his expectations will be of you. Remember this book is centered around women seeking traditional marriage, where the man is the head. There are some men that have a very cavalier attitude about finances, relationships, and their responsibility to the household. Some men believe in the 50/50 principle, some women are fine with that, others feel it's akin to being a roommate. If one party has good credit and the other has a bad track record, how will this be taken care of in the future? What if both parties aren't that great with money matters, can this union stand a chance? If you happen to meet a man that has significant assets, will you be okay signing a prenup? What are your views on joint bank accounts? Have these discussions sooner than later, as this is one of the top causes of the breakdown in marriage.

Health

The topic of health is one of the most vitally important topics today. A person's outlook on their health is tied to their value system, why? Our bodies are our temples. How we take care of our temples is an indication of how we treat ourselves, and possibly how we will treat others. I will tell you, ladies, many men who have taken on a healthy lifestyle will not compromise in this area and vice versa. No matter how old school it seems, for the most part, women are responsible for the nutrition in the home. If the woman is preparing healthy meals and the husband is against it, that poses a great problem as well as the reverse.

Then there is a great divide over homeopathic medicines as opposed to treatments with pharmaceuticals. I know several couples who were completely at odds, over the Covid-19 vaccinations, one spouse was for, one spouse against. The houses were further split when it came to children. Health, eating habits, weight, sickness, and mental fitness are all very important values we should hold dear. The topic of weight is always a sensitive issue. While there will always be opinions about what is physically attractive to a person, we cannot ignore that diets and obesity are leading causes for most diseases. Many people view a person's lack of discipline to control their eating habits and weight, as a very strong indication of this person's value system. Do you or your potential spouse have expectations for maintaining a certain weight? What will happen when someone misses the mark? Among the topic of diet, the vegan lifestyle is gaining popularity. Dating a vegan or non-vegan when you are the opposite, is more than a little challenging. A person's outlook on health is a value system that ranks quite high when considering a quality mate.

Respect

Give me just a little bit? No, give me a lot. Respect is often equated to name-calling and yelling. Beneath the surface, it runs much deeper. A woman may have experienced an absent or abusive father growing up;

therefore, her view of men is not a healthy one. If a man had a toxic relationship with his mother or mother figure, his overall outlook on womanhood will not be positive. Respect also reaches into areas of beliefs, opinions, and lifestyles. A musician that makes a living from gig to gig, may not be taken seriously by their mate. Therefore, their gig work won't be respected on the same level as a corporate 9-5. If a woman doesn't respect her husband as the head of the home, she may take the lead, ignore, and flat our disregard decisions he has made. That is disrespect in many instances to his manhood. As a reminder, this book is specifically written for marriage-minded singles seeking the traditional roles of husband and wife.

In today's culture, name-calling can be a term of endearment, but this is a slippery slope. Does your man casually call women out of their names? Do you often do this with men? I don't mean a particular instance, does he or you regularly have negative connotations when it comes to the opposite sex? Is he respectful to women? Does he know how to talk to you? Does he have a good relationship with his children? Does he have a good work ethic, or does he just do enough to get by? Does he respect his place of business or employment? Respect goes a long way and should be a major determining factor in determining compatibility.

> These are just a few. Values are key. Just make sure you have the same values you expect in him!

6

Influencers

"Enjoy each other without the opinions and validation of social media."

A relationship is between two people, right? Explain then, why are so many people able to have an opinion about your relationship? Do you realize some women, simply cannot maintain a relationship because of their circle of influence? Some things you've allowed in the past, some behaviors you may not be conscious of. Examine the influencers in your life, they may have been secretly holding you back from your soulmate.

Friends

Your friends should NEVER go on dates with you and your potential mate, talk to him on the phone about your relationship or address him in any way, shape, or form. This is not only downright disrespectful but also immature and screams that you are a drama queen! Your relationship is your business. Also, if you stop telling them every single detail of your relationship, they wouldn't have so many opinions. Friends can only comment about what you tell them. If a friend is overly inquisitive, that may be a problem as well. Are your friends in healthy relationships? If your friend is always in dysfunctional situations, they may take out their personal frustrations on your life. This can also happen with married friends that are unhappy.

Unless there is any type of abuse or criminal behavior, even infidelity! It's not your friend's place to instruct you on how to handle your love life. Many of your friends may still be living out their youth, not value relationships, or your new life. A friend that also demands your time when you are seriously seeing someone, isn't mature enough to understand, your life is different. They haven't disconnected from the times when you were single and mingling. This is very serious, evaluate your circle of influence carefully. It could literally make or break a perfectly healthy relationship.

Children

This is quite a tricky one. A child can pretend not to like a potential suitor just because they either want you to themselves, or they want you to get back with their father. Children, I don't care what age, should never have a say in your relationship, ever! If you have underage children, you of course want to observe their interactions with him, but that is it. I would also advise until you know this man well, do not introduce him to your children. This can be especially bad for mothers and sons. Your son is not your husband! Do not allow him to have any say or authority over your personal life. A mother may call her son, KING and the "man of the house." How do you think the son will feel when there is a new King in town? Be very careful with this. Moms, let me give you a piece of reality. Have an opinion about your children's (teen or adult) relationship and they will quickly usher you out of their business, with no problem! You should return the energy! Having children in adult affairs, no matter their ages can pose a major issue in a relationship.

Social Media

Question? What reason do you have to post about a new relationship? Ever? Think about it for one moment. The only reason, is to show others you have someone, make an ex jealous, or prove to any women he may have around that he is taken. When I tell you, I have rarely seen these scenarios turn out good. I address this in my mini-series FAKERS. Your private life is just that, private. You should NEVER ask a man to post you on his page or even connect you with an "in a relationship with" tag. This does absolutely nothing but fuel gossip. If there's a breakup, you must explain to your whole timeline what happened. It's honestly immature.

Get to know your man, just you and he, let the rest work itself out. Enjoy each other without the opinions and validation of social media. I know grown women who have ended relationships with men because they refused to post them on social media. As if, men that have their women fully posted on social media, aren't sliding in other women's inboxes and DMs? Social media proves nothing and should not be used as a measuring stick for how solid your relationship is. Mature men are discreet and so are wise women.

Parents

This is the most difficult one and if you don't nip it in the bud, it will be death to all your relationships. This problem is typically centered around mothers. Fathers may have opinions, but they tend to keep them in a private setting. I have heard nightmare stories. Such as someone's mother demanding money, asking inappropriate questions, intruding on dates, having ridiculous opinions, and flat-out destroying relationships on purpose. In many of these instances, the mother's personal life is out of order. I have grown daughters and I do none of the sorts. While we value our parents' opinions and want their approval, keep them at a distance. You also need clear boundaries as to what and what is not appropriate. Know your parents, we all didn't come from healthy homes, all parents aren't solid, mature, and grounded people. If you know your parents are grounded and wise, you may want to consider rigorously what they think of your new boo. Parents should always be honored in any instance and their opinion valued; however, your parents should not be expressing this to your mate directly.

Siblings

Siblings can be an extension of the parents' disapproval. Siblings also tend to take private information and share it with the rest of the family. Siblings can literally make your dating life hell, especially if there is an undercurrent of sibling rivalry, envy, or loneliness. The same advice applies, value their opinion but place strict boundaries on their communication with your man and limit what you share.

Relationship Experts

Yes! Too many women follow to a tee, what a celebrity expert says about a relationship. I will admit, a lot of the information is great, however, you should never measure your relationship by the stick of a so-called relationship expert. I've seen people literally start arguments, have suspicions, and put trouble in their relationship, all from a five-minute YouTube tutorial (i.e., 5 Signs to know he is the One).

Influencers can kill your relationship before it even gets started. We put too many people in our private lives and for a mature man, this is a major violation. A man needs to know that his secrets and private information are safe with you. Before you blast your new man on the gram, brag to friends, parents, or look for the approval of children, how about you get to know him and judge for yourself?

7

Red Flags

"The absolute #1 Red Flag is now, and always will be, IN-CONSISTENCY."

Now that you have met this great guy, whether it was at Starbucks, while you were hitting the elliptical, or during a Facebook chat, this is the make-or-break moment for both of you. What do people do when they first meet? They put their best foot forward. If you let everyone tell it, they are in a great place in their life, with great health, a great career, A1 credit, and a luxury home. Most of the time, that is the furthest thing from the truth!

It's important during the "getting to know you phase" that you are relaxed and at ease. But it's also a time to pay attention—close attention.

#1 Red Flag: Inconsistency

I can't scream this loud enough girlfriend. The absolute #1 red flag is now, and always will be, INCONSISTENCY. It's not rocket science at all to identify inconsistency.

- Do his actions line up with his words?
- Is he a man of his word?
- Does he call when he says he will?

- If he can't call, does he at least text and say he is tied up?
- Do you find inconsistencies in his stories? One minute he has been divorced five years, the next it's barely one.
- Does he break dates and change plans often?
- Does he go MIA during certain times, like after work, during the day, or on weekends?
- Does he make promises he can't keep? Do you have to constantly remind him of things he said he would do? I used to talk to a guy during his lunch break and after work, but never at night and rarely on the weekend. It was no big deal at first because we talked often. It turned out that those dark times, were because he was at home with his live-in girlfriend! Now back to our regularly scheduled program!
- Does he pop in and out of your life or in today's terms, does he GHOST YOU? Is he inconsistent about his life, career, and relationship or details of his schedule? These are major red flags and, honestly, I don't care how good of a catch he seems to be or how much of a connection you all have.

These are causes to bail, and bail immediately. Chances are, if you confront him about the inconsistencies, he will just tell another lie to cover it up. An inconsistent man is also one you can't count on, not husband material.

#2 Red Flag: Bitter Brian

What's his overall attitude toward women? Is he bitter and angry at an ex? If he constantly talks about how she hurt him, this man is damaged and will do nothing but damage you. You cannot save him. This is a major red flag. Give him Iyanla's phone number so she can "Fix His Life" because he will do nothing but mess up yours, and then you will be the one calling Iyanla!

#3 Red Flag: Isolation

Is everyone against him? You ever met a person that has a problem with everyone? They are on the outs with family, friends, and even co-workers? While we all have our share of problems with people if every-one is his enemy and against him, I would say, ladies, this is a major red flag. Don't fall for the banana-in-the-tailpipe, and believe you are the only one that understands him. Furthermore, if you feel like everyone is a hater, jealous and you can't keep any real friends, you have a bigger problem on your hands than finding a man.

#4 Red Flag: Broke

Quite simply, if you are on a date and he forgot his wallet, asks you for gas money, asks you to let him "hold something," it's a red flag. If he asks you to cosign on a car or put a utility bill in your name before you even know his last name, call Houston, because you have a problem! Respectable men don't ask women for money. End of story.

#5 Red Flag: Secrets

If you are seeing someone for a significant amount of time, and he never introduces you to his family or friends, this is a major warning sign. This person is married or possibly not taking the relationship as seriously as you are. It's hard to state when it's a good time to meet someone's family, but if you are not familiar with anyone in his circle, this is cause for major red *flaggage!*

#6 Red Flag: Schemers

There are a lot of schemers out here. They have money-making schemes, and they are looking for your money or credit to carry it out. Do not, for any reason, let a man have your personal information or do anything that even seems slightly suspicious to you. Never give a man money for a business venture without thoroughly researching it. Just be careful. Some schemers prey on single women that have the means to help them get their end.

#7 Red Flag: Disrespectful

These go hand in hand. A man that is rude and unkind to you is going to eventually be disrespectful to you. Does he treat you like a lady? Does he curse, raise his voice at you or hang up the phone when he doesn't get his way? Does he make dates and stand you up? Does he gawk at other women when you are in public? Is he rude to serving staff? Sweetheart, you have a real live douche bag on your hands. Unless you want to deal with that for the duration of your relationship, I suggest you flush the toilet of this waste of time.

Men's Red Flags

We conducted a poll of deal-breakers for both married and single men from ages 25-65. Surprisingly, the results were standard across age and relationship gaps.

Vulgar Women

Without a doubt, this was the top red flag for the men we polled. Honestly, this woman should be a red flag for anyone! Specifics were profane vocabulary, public drunkenness, loudness, disrespectful to family. The men were very big on down talking, cursing, and yelling at children. A woman that is all-around argumentative, and combative.

Obsessed with an Ex

Women who constantly talk about, bash, and bring up their ex and the history of their ex. No man wants to hear about your ex. No man wants you to be in his presence but your mind is on another man. Also, the way she talks about her ex will probably be how she talks about him. The men are clear, she's not over her ex but they are over her!

Forcing Relationships

Women that try to force exclusivity and talk about commitment, sometimes a few weeks or even days at the start of dating! Men were clear, these women don't know them nor had tried to get to know them. These women simply wanted a relationship and felt entitled to it. Especially after being intimate early on, these women demanded commitment.

An honorable mention goes to women that are *Drama Queens.* There you have it from the men!

> Never ignore red flags. Many make the mistake of downplaying a red flag to a yellow flag (proceed with caution) under the guise of giving people the benefit of the doubt. Maya Angelou famously stated, "When someone shows you who they are, believe them the first time." People aren't perfect, but there are just some behaviors you should not entertain.

8

No Scrubs

"The man that you will consider marrying will not necessarily be perfect, but he should have stability in income, finances, and residence."

That song is in my rotation. I love it! I know all the lyrics and the dance routine from the video! "No Scrubs" by TLC was then, and still is now a woman's anthem. Slow down, before you get too excited, we are not talking about the context of the song. No ma'am! This is about why women choose scrubs!

Kelly met a man named Jim. He was very tall, about 6'7", and very big in stature, but not very attractive. Kelly had recently experienced some tragedy in her life. She lost money due to a bad investment, had to downsize her apartment, and broke up with her boyfriend of five years. Kelly was downright depressed. Kelly met Jim at a gas station and proceeded to make out with him in her car, yes, that day! Kelly did not know this man's last name, date of birth, or marital status. Well after the steamy make-out session, they exchanged numbers.

Kelly soon found out that Jim was a recovering crack addict living in a homeless shelter. You read that correctly! Kelly for some reason made this man a project, she bought him to church with her, even let him meet her family. Jim had a low-paying job and they decided they had enough money to move in together.

Jim was never mean, unkind, or disrespectful to Kelly, he was actually a very nice man trying to get his life together. Then one day, he just stopped calling. Kelly was relieved he stopped communicating, she knew in her heart this relationship wasn't right for her. At the time, Kelly was so low in life, she lied to herself and tried to make this man and this relationship much more than what it was. Yes, ladies, Kelly was dating a SCRUB. It's not about us seeing the best in a man or helping a man when he is down. The man that you will consider marrying will not necessarily be perfect, but he should have stability in income, finances, and residence. If you are constantly drawn to men that need help getting fixed up or picked up, the reason may be because that is all you think you deserve. If it's meant to be, allow the man to get grounded and revisit it later. If not, you may be in for a life of unnecessary struggle.

Have women been involved with men that transformed from scrubs to responsible men, yes? But it's a gamble. A rule of thumb is accepting people where they are knowing they may never change. If you are okay with that, then proceed with great caution.

9

Wolf in Sheep's Clothing

> "A wolf initially may seem like an answer to prayer, right before it devours you. "

A wolf is a predator. If you saw a wolf, you would automatically take off running. They are vicious killers out for prey. For a wolf to get close to his target, he disguises himself as the meekest, mildest animal of them all—a sheep. Sheep are sweet, loving and kind. Who would be afraid of cute little sheep? A wolf initially may seem like an answer to prayer, right before it devours you.

Shannon met Chris while at a business conference out of town. Upon meeting, it was an instant, almost electric attraction. He was professional, well-groomed, well-spoken, and he had an amazing smile! After the conference, they made plans to go to dinner. Chris treated Shannon to dinner at a nice restaurant and they had an amazing conversation. The night was far spent, so Chris invited Shannon to spend the night at his home, due to the lateness of the hour. Shannon was very offended, and Chris apologized. Little did she know, his wolf was coming out. However, his charm was electric and instead of spending the night with him, she invited him to her hotel. Oh, Shannon!

Chris and Shannon spent the weekend together and he treated her to every meal and even introduced her to some of his friends and took her to his place of worship. Chris was not only well-educated and a career man, but he was a senior pastor. He was fine, smart, and spiritual. Can you say fairy tale?

Within a week, Chris met Shannon's family and even her family agreed, he was the one. Things were off on the fast track. Chris was so charming and never ever let Sandy touch a bill while out on the town. That first week of courtship seemed like heaven. And as fate would have it, that first week of their relationship was the best.

Although Sandy and Chris lived in different cities, they kept in touch often. But she started to notice something, every time they talked, she felt bad. Not bad about the distance but bad about herself. Things progressively worsened. Everything she said, he turned it around and somehow, she was a bad person. He was a master at Jedi Mind tricks. This is what I reference as the technique of the predator wolf. According to starwars.com, Jedi Mind Tricks are the implanting of suggestions in the minds of those the Jedi encounters, these suggestions, encourage them to comply with the Jedi's wishes. This technique is a slow leak that can even fool the savviest of individuals.

Once, he broke up with Shannon during an out-of-town visit. He said Shannon needed to grow and evolve to be ready and prepared for him in the future. He touted that she was not mentally, emotionally, or spiritually mature enough for a man of his stature, so he decided to put the relationship on "ice".

He once told Shannon because she did not graduate from college, and he had a master's degree, she was beneath him, but he would talk on her level so she could understand. He would scold Shannon. And then a bombshell came, he told Shannon that he could never marry her because she was a loose woman, who slept with him on the first date and had children out of wedlock. He broke Shannon down in every way possible. Chris was majorly verbally abusive and after a while, Shannon knew he would have been physically abusive.

How could someone so seemingly right initially, be so wrong? The clues were there, from the first date. Also, Shannon had to hold herself responsible as well. Ladies, I don't care what anyone tells you, or what experiences others have. Do not sleep with a man on the first date, we will deal with this later, but just don't do it. Chris was a dream that became a nightmare. In between the mind manipulation and constant critique of her life, he would buy gifts and do many "romantic" gestures. Shannon got out just in time. Chris married a younger woman, right after they broke up, and she made police reports that he was physically abusive.

Remember, a wolf is a predator. It has a target to destroy and prey to annihilate. When you see "wolf" tendencies, run as fast as you can, before you are the next victim.

10

When in Doubt Check
Them Out

> "Should you research someone you're dating? Is it an invasion of
> their privacy? Well, yes, it is, but are you more concerned about
> their privacy or your well-being?"

D o me a favor right now. Search your name, using your name, city,
and state, and tell me what comes up? Also, search earth or satel-
lite maps with your address. The results are scary, aren't they? Those
are just free results from an internet search. Fee-based services can re-
veal everything from current address, phone number, employment,
criminal history, relatives, marriage, and divorce records, and annual
salary, for starters. The more extensive searches range in price from
$2-$50, depending on the type and extension of background you need.

How does this relate to dating? Should you research someone you're
dating? Is it an invasion of their privacy? Well, yes, it is, but are you
more concerned about their privacy or your well-being? When I tell
you about an experience with two men I met, Mario and David, you
will see why. While seriously dating, you need to know who is going
to be in your space, your home, around your children, and in your life
period.

Case of Mario

Mario was in his mid-forties and was a very hard-working man. He had four children, two that were in college and two who lived with him. He was very mild-mannered and spiritual. He was a breath of fresh air from the normal, borderline arrogant guys, I had been dating.

Our first few dates went well, and we seemed to hit it off. As things got serious, I decided to do a free search on him. To do a search, you need the person's first and last legal name, their age and date of birth, and their current city and state. These are things we should know within the first one or two dates anyway. I conducted the search and sure enough, his name and statistics came back. I felt at ease with him. But as I kept scrolling, I saw something that made my eyes bulge! It was a wedding website with his picture, a middle-aged woman, and wedding date that was projected about 18 months from the current date. I was beyond livid! Mario explained to me that he was previously engaged. However, he said the engagement was broken because his ex-fiancé did not want school-aged children.

It could have been a lie. But I had been over his house several times and met his children. I had been to his place of employment, place of worship and met a few of his acquaintances. I was confident that what he told me was true.

As time went on, our relationship was lukewarm at best. Our schedules were hectic, and it was frustrating, so I decided to end it. He then dropped a bombshell on me. He said that he had congestive heart failure and had a pacemaker that needed replacement. Sure enough, he put my hand over his heart, and I felt it.

When we first started seeing each other, Mario invited me to his 25th class reunion in California. I was looking forward to it because I had never been out west. So as the date got closer, we never solidified any plans. Things got complicated because he had a minor surgical procedure right before the reunion. I was sure he wasn't going to travel anywhere.

During and after his surgery, Mario didn't want me to see him. I understood, so I stood back and gave him space. But to my surprise, shortly after his surgery, he told me he was on the way to California. He said his aunt had fallen ill and didn't have much time left. He said he would try his best to get me a ticket to join him. That was on a Thursday. I didn't really talk to him at all until Friday, at which time he said the tickets were just too high. They were $700. So, I digressed.

I went to bed that next Saturday night and I couldn't rest. It's like my spirit was tossing and turning. So, I literally got up and went to the computer. I searched Mario's name again and the same information came up, including the website for his broken engagement. I then did a search on his ex-fiancé. Not only did her name, age, and address come up, but so did a phone number. It was about 2 a.m., but something in me needed answers. I called the phone number privately and she answered.

- "Hello, may I speak with Angie?"
- "This is Angie. Who is this, may I ask?"
- "I'd rather not give my name, but do you know Mario?"
- "Yes, I do," she said. "What is this about?"
- "Mario and I have been dating the past few months, but there are some things not adding up."
- The phone went silent. Then, as the Gap Band says, she dropped the bomb on me.
- "Dating? We are getting married next week on Friday in Reno; Nevada and I'm going to his class reunion."

I was beyond words. Where was she? I told her I was at his house all the time, spending time with his children. I told her that I'd been to his job and even social events where I met his boss. We swapped stories, and she said revealed she was with him during his hospital stay. Suddenly, it all added up. She told me that their engagement was off. I felt so bad for her, not for me at the time.

That's not the end! After a bunch of yelling, finger-pointing, and emotional arguments, he called and said he really needed to explain everything. I was baffled, how could this be? A tell-tell sign of cheating is never being invited over to your companion's house or being introduced to their family, right? This was not the case here at all!

He then dropped bombs five, six, and seven on me. In a nutshell, Mario said that he had very little time to live. With his children's mother being terminally ill (this was true) and him having primary custody, he needed to be around for his children, but he didn't have insurance (I didn't know that, but it was true). He said that Angie was a nice lady, and they hit it off in the beginning. But they were from two different worlds. She was a very successful, high-level insurance adjuster, for a major company. He was marrying her, for the benefits primarily, and they had no plans to even live together. He planned to stay in his home, and she would stay in hers. No one knew about their engagement, not even his children. This was more so an arrangement. And a weird one, I might add. But now that she had broken off the engagement, he didn't know what he was going to do.

Wowzers! And wowzers again! My mind was all over the place. I had never been so deceived and lied to in my entire life. Our whole relationship was a lie. Had I just broken it off in the beginning, after discovering his engagement website, I would have avoided all this drama?

Fast forward to the next Saturday. It was the day of his reunion, but it was also a wedding anniversary of a friend. I hadn't heard from him, so I didn't know if he was back home or not. Once again, my spirit was restless. So, I took to the Internet once again. This time, I went to his class reunion Facebook page. And then boom! There it was plain as day: a picture of Mario and Angela with the caption, "Congrats to Mario and his bride of one day, Angela!" They did it. They got married anyway! Mario was honest about one thing, they maintained separate homes, even after the marriage. Had I not researched and found out what I did, he would have never informed me that he was engaged or married. He lived life as a single man, both during his engagement and after his wedding.

Case of David

Eventually, I met a different type of gentleman, and gentleman he was! David was every bit of 6'5" and 370 pounds. He was very intellectual and smart, but with an edge to him. I decided to check out his Facebook page. Sure enough, while the profile name said David, the actual URL or link name said Carl. Maybe he was using his middle name, and that was fine. But I searched deeper. Bam, there it was! A search under the name Carl revealed he had an arrest record and a suspended driver's license. Why a high-level financial manager, at a prestigious law firm, was driving around on a suspended license, was beyond comprehension. It wasn't really a deal-breaker; it was just time for a serious conversation.

David was a single dad, living in a very affluent part of town with a property on the lake. He had never been married (so he said) and his children were teens. So oddly enough, a court document came up with his name on it. As I read the document, I was in utter disbelief and fear. David, Carl, whatever his name was, was accused of murdering his wife nearly ten years ago, bragging about it in jail, and literally got away with murder! He was acquitted of all charges, but something in me felt that although he got away with it, he was guilty. He was an ex-military officer and retired high-level law enforcement agent. He even told me that he could get rid of someone and not get caught!

So just to be sure this wasn't a big mistake because murder is not something to sweep over lightly, I then took it a bit further. I paid for an extensive search. I discovered court documents that had the deceased wife's name and date of birth. When you pay for an extensive search, it shows you who the person could be related to. Sure enough, on his file, it stated that he was related to this deceased woman, same age, same date of birth, and same address.

At a minimum, he lied about being married and I see why. I was scared. I broke things off with him (not telling him why) and he was still being persistent about seeing me. Of course, a little fear and panic set in. But I had a few friends and family in law enforcement. They were aware of my situation and coached me on how to handle him.

What would have happened if I didn't search for more information on David and Mario? Would my life be in danger? Would I be involved in a potentially crazy love triangle that could have gone violent? These men were pretending to be something that they were not. And do I feel even slightly guilty for invading their privacy; no, I do not! I would not get upset if a potential mate did a search (and an extensive one) on me. I have nothing to hide. In this case, thank God I checked, these background checks could have saved my life.

11

Keep Your Panties On

"Keep your panties on and your calendar open!"

Y es, it means just what the title says. Ladies, keep your panties on for as long as you can! We have grown women! Let's face it! Grown women are sexually active for the most part. Neither I nor anyone else is here to tell you what to do with your bodies. Your choice, your pleasure or pain, your consequence. Let's not be foolish and Uber religious to think that most people are going to abstain. It sounds good on paper, but it's not happening. Now, your religious beliefs or personal convictions may have you celibate at this time in your life, and that is wonderful.

This is not about playing hard to get. This is solely about you! This is about getting to know someone in a deep, intimate way. This is about developing a friendship that lasts. This is about making non-physical connections. It's powerful! If you have never tried it, it's transformative! It shows you respect yourself and have high values.

While the absence of sex doesn't make a man marry you, neither does being intimate with a man deter him, if you are truly the woman he wants. Most people that are married have been intimate sexually. Let's not be naïve and delusional about this. But keeping your legs closed, ladies, let a man make love to your heart and your mind before he ever touches your body. If you want something different, do something dif-

65

ferent. For many ladies, that means getting a chastity belt because your *legs open faster than the gates at a horse race...*

Keep Your Options Open

Dating comes with a lot of unnecessary heartbreak. We treat the dating phase as if it's a committed, exclusive relationship, or we get into an exclusive relationship before we really know the person at all.

Just because a man demands or expects you to be exclusive immediately, doesn't mean you have to be. Neither one of you knows each other or knows if the relationship will work. Date, and date multiple people if the opportunity arises. Most men date multiple women, and ladies, they are not players! You say they are players because you are only dating him, and you expect him to do the same. When you find out that's not the case, your heart is broken, more so because you let him open the cookie jar on a regular.

It's important that we allow people to create their own stories. It's important to know there are exceptions. You could go on one date with someone, and you all talk for hours and hours. By the end of the date, you both agree to see each other exclusively. But if the man you are seeing has never brought that up, instead of talking to him every other minute about when the relationship is going to the next level, enjoy your time with him. If someone else wants to take you out, go. Keeping your options open means you are not settling.

If you are keeping your legs closed, but keeping your options open, eventually, someone will see your worth and he won't want you to see another man. Until then, keep your panties on and your calendar open! Enjoy yourself!

12

Treat Her Like a Lady

> "If a man must do too much work to get to know you, he will easily go to the next person that may be "less" qualified than you, but is open."

Contrary to popular belief, 26" designer hair extensions, the latest Louis Vuitton bag and the newest collection of Louboutin's (red bottoms in the popular vernacular) do not make one a lady. What is a lady? How does she carry herself? More importantly, how does it factor into dating? A lady is classy. She is witty, smart, honest, and self-assured. She is not perfect, but perfectly secure in her imperfections. She understands that although her accomplishments are many, she does not have to carry herself nor behave like her male counterparts to compete in the marketplace. A lady isn't weak; she is strong. She understands that her strength is from her God-given ability to be the carrier of life. A lady is a nurturer. She understands that her strength is in her femininity.

A lady is not loud, rude, lewd, abrasive, profane, argumentative, or combative. Do we all have our moments? Of course! But a lady understands that she can draw more flies with honey, and she chooses her battles and her words wisely. A lady is a work in progress. A lady is ever-evolving, desiring to improve herself daily. To sum it up, a lady is an example to the younger women, to daughters and nieces.

Does a lady stumble out of the club, sloppy drunk, or does she know her limits? Does she yell, scream, curse, and throw up gang signs in public, acting a pure fool? Does she twerk on social media and in public places and wear bonnets and pajamas out of the house? Absolutely not! Although a lady is more than her attire, she will never be inappropriate. What's sad is that so many images in the media now depict women, especially women of color, as anything but lady-like. Beautiful, well-dressed women with the perfect hair, shape, and makeup open their mouths and all you hear is a beep every 10 seconds.

We are all adults here. You have a right to live the way you want. But what is your behavior saying about you? What is the perception of your personality based on your actions? It seems the order of the day is speaking loudly and saying nothing. A lady doesn't speak loudly or harshly. She understands the texture of her voice is alluring and she speaks as such.

It's not easy, ladies. So many of us have had to raise children without the presence of a father. We work careers and go to school. We struggle financially and emotionally. Many women had to do it all, with little or no help. Let's not even talk about the heartbreak and pain of various relationships, it's made us tough. No one can come in, and you aren't letting anything out. Many women seem to be defensive and combative. Love requires opening your heart, at the same time, guarding your heart. Be open, not foolish.

Women that have their hearts open are attractive to men. If a man must do too much work to get to know you, he will easily go to the next person that may be "less" qualified than you but is open. That's what a lot of my sisters don't understand. A man is looking for a lady, a soft spot to lay his head after a long day. He needs loving words of comfort, but strength and compassion, to see him through tough times. A man will shut down when you show signs of aggression and harshness. Many of you do this because you are treating him like your ex or the last few losers you have dated.

But ladies, and ladies in the making, you will never get anywhere like that. Be vulnerable! Yes, I said vulnerable! Be vulnerable to the process of getting to know another person. But also use the wisdom of your years and life experience to see red flags and warning signs.

Quite simply, a lady knows her strengths and embraces her weaknesses. She understands her role and cherishes it. A lady is, quite simply, the greatest gift a man can ever find. She is a true treasure.

13

Side Chicks

"The lips that kiss the side chick, also kiss the wife..."

The television series SCANDAL portrayed Kerry Washington's character "Olivia", as the powerful side chick to the President. She was shown to be a hero of sorts, who in the end, won. This gave side chicks all over the world, false hope, and confidence! Some women get into these relationships with full knowledge and acceptance that this man is married. A few, however, are tricked, lied to, and deceived about men's marital status. Although, as previously stated, a quick background check would remedy this immediately, I digress.

Every woman I know that is a side chick, is taken care of financially. Not just gifts, but up to and including, having all her living expenses paid for in totality. For the most part, they are treated well (as if being someone's option is treating you well, but I digress). Believe it or not, some side chicks even get some time on holidays and have met their man's family and even his children.

Is this what you want for your life? Is this the life you would want for your daughters? Is this an example to show your sons? Why are you putting up with this? There are a million reasons people end up being the side chick. Sometimes, the man has told them he was divorcing or was in the middle of divorce proceedings. By the time the truth comes out, the woman's feelings and in many instances, her livelihood is involved, and it's hard to just end it. Anyone that says it's easy, isn't being honest.

Don't believe the hype. There are plenty of good men out there. If you aren't meeting them, maybe you are not what they are looking for! But don't blame the lack of good men on your reason for being the side chick. Don't get so caught up in the money that he spends, that you are blinded to what is really going on.

Come on, girlfriend! How long are you going to be his option? And better yet, how would you feel if you were the wife? Please don't believe him! Don't believe that the marriage is bad, and you are good. Don't believe that when he leaves her, he is going to marry you. Could it happen? Yes. Have I seen it happen? Yes. Will it happen? Probably not! There is an old saying and principle: Do unto others as you would have them do unto you. Many side chicks believe, because she hasn't taken any vows, she has no culpability in the situation. Shouldn't we be our sisters' keepers? All married men claim they don't sleep with their wives when they have a side chick. They make her believe she's the object of their desire, and they are no longer attracted to their wives. But they are lying.

The lips that kiss the side chick, also kiss the wife. I can only imagine, where else his mouth has been... Usually, you are not the only one. Ironically, side chicks expect these lying cheaters to be faithful to them. This madness has got to end! Men only do what we allow them to do. So how would you feel if your husband was sneaking, creeping, slobbering, and spending household money on another chick? Not so fun when the rabbits' got the gun, huh?

Do your self-esteem a favor and don't let it be bought, used, and dragged along! But until you find your worth, know who you are and what you have to offer. Don't contribute to a man's infidelity. You will most likely repeat this pattern until, of course, he leaves his wife, marries you, and then your position of the side chick is now open to another. If he, did it to her, he will most likely do it to you, with no conscious thought or effort. So now, is that really a good man, or will you open your eyes as Whitney Houston did in "Waiting to Exhale" to realize that her man was the scum of the earth?

14

Baby Mama

> "Think of how your interaction with your children's father looks to a potential."

Are you a crazy baby mama? You read that right! I'm not asking if you are dating a man with a crazy baby mama; I'm asking are you one? Do you unnecessarily harass your ex and give him a hard time about his children? Are you unrealistic and demanding? Have you made this man's life a living hell? I hear you saying, "You don't know what he did to me. He is not here for these kids. He is a deadbeat." He may be those things, but why are you letting his behavior, make you act in an unflattering way? Does your behavior make you *good-man repellant?* No quality man is going to be bothered with a woman that is in constant drama with her child's father. He's looking at how you may be with him or around his children. He will NEVER be with you if you withhold visitation from the natural father of your children. Good men hate drama. They hate it. Especially from ex-wives and their children's mothers. Just remember, it's not about what someone does to you; it's how you react to it. Work out that bitterness and anger.

Baby Mama (never married)

I understand that many of you loved and had children with a man, that you never married. Perhaps you parted on amicable terms or maybe you never had a relationship, to begin with. In either case, raising children without their father in the home, with (possibly) little to no help, is a devastating life event for any mother. It's important to note, there are many fathers that actively support, co-parent, and have full custody of their children. Although that may or may not be your experience, great dads exist, in great numbers. Nevertheless, the plight of single families comes with some serious stressors according to The American Psychological Association.

Single Family Stressors

- Visitation and custody problems. (Families: Single Parenting and Today's Family, 2019)
- The effects of the continuing conflict between the parents. (Families: Single Parenting and Today's Family, 2019)
- Less opportunity for parents and children to spend time together.(Families: Single Parenting and Today's Family, 2019)
- Effects of the breakup on children's school performance and peer relations. (Families: Single Parenting and Today's Family, 2019)
- Disruptions of extended family relationships. (Families: Single Parenting and Today's Family, 2019)
- Problems caused by the parents' dating and entering new relationships. (Families: Single Parenting and Today's Family, 2019)

Children growing up without a father in the home is more devastating than you think. The data is startling.

Children without Fathers in the Home

- Twenty-five million children are growing up without fathers in the home. That's 40% of the kids in America. (U.S. Single Family Households, 2012)
- 40% of all live births in the US are to single mothers. (U.S. Single Family Households, 2012)

- 90% of welfare recipients are single mothers. (U.S. Single Family Households, 2012)
- 70% of gang members, high school dropouts, teen suicides, teen pregnancies, and teen substance abusers come from single-mother homes. (U.S. Single Family Households, 2012)
- Statistically, a child in a single-parent household is far more likely to experience violence, commit suicide, continue a cycle of poverty, become drug dependent, commit a crime, or perform below his peers in education.(U.S. Single-Family Households, 2012)
- Thirty-seven percent of families led by single mothers nation-wide live-in poverty. Comparatively, only 6.8% of families with married parents live in poverty. (U.S. Single Family Households, 2012)
- 63% of youth suicides. (U.S. Single Family Households, 2012)
- 90% of all homeless and runaway children .(U.S. Single-Family Households, 2012)
- 85% of all children that exhibit behavioral disorders. (U.S. Single Family Households, 2012)
- 80% of rapists are motivated by displaced anger. (U.S. Single Family Households, 2012)
- 71% of all high school dropouts. (U.S. Single Family Households, 2012)
- 75% of all adolescent patients in chemical abuse centers. (U.S. Single Family Households, 2012)
- 70% of juveniles in state-operated institutions (U.S. Single-Family Households, 2012)
- 85% of all youths sitting in prisons (U.S. Single-Family Households, 2012)

This may take a moment to digest. The rate of single mothers giving birth now surpasses the rate of babies born to married couples, especially in the African American Community. We cannot ignore the devastation this has caused. This information is not to shock you, it's to educate. I was a young single mother; I wish this information was available to me back then. These startling statistics are to make parents aware, there are underline behaviors your children may have, despite giving them the best life you possibly can. What does this have to do with dating? Absolutely everything. Introducing a man into your already complicated family unit is no small feat. It's complicated for the children as well as all adults involved.

Baby Mama (divorced)

Dating after divorce with minor children is a challenge in and of itself. Find a way to work peaceably with your children's father. Even if he is the biggest jerk in the world, don't let that jerk turn you into his female predecessor. Assuming that you are not just a drama queen by nature, think of how your interaction with your ex-husband looks to a potential mate. Not too hot right? Learn how to handle and control your emotions. Please do not talk bad about your ex to your new man. It's a definite turn-off! Now if you are a *baby mama* by divorce, the data on divorced parents and their children are just as, if not more startling, than the data on single-parent homes.

Children of Divorced Parents

- Diminishing the child's future competence. (Anderson, 2014)
- Contributing to early sexual experimentation leading to increased costs for society. (Anderson, 2014)
- Adversely affecting religious practice—divorce diminishes the frequency of religious worship. (Anderson, 2014)
- Diminishing a child's learning capacity and educational attainment.(Anderson, 2014)
- Increasing crime rates and substance use, with associated societal and governmental costs. (Anderson, 2014)
- Increasing risk for school suspensions. (Anderson, 2014)

- Increasing emotional and mental health risks, including suicide. (Anderson, 2014)
- The child may change his or her outlook on sexual behavior.(Anderson, 2014)
- There is increased approval (by children of divorced parents) of premarital sex, cohabitation, and divorce.(Anderson, 2014)
- There is an earlier sexual debut. (Anderson, 2014)
- Girls whose fathers left the home before they were five years old were eight times more likely to become pregnant as adolescents than girls from intact families.(Anderson, 2014)
- Boys similarly have earlier sexual debut and higher rates of sexually transmitted disease when they have experienced divorce in their family. (Anderson, 2014)

Divorcing is a major life occurrence that society greatly underplays. Most married women, I'm positive, didn't enter their union, imagining it would end in divorce. Most divorced women, never imagined, they would not have a man in the home for their children. I think we are so numb to the word *divorce*; we forget how traumatic it is for the adults involved.

Divorced Men and Women

- Half of the women and one-third of the men were still very angry with their former spouses.(Anderson, 2014)
- One-third of the women and one-fourth of the men felt that life was unfair and disappointing.(Anderson, 2014)
- In only 10 percent of divorces did both partners feel they achieved happier lives.(Anderson, 2014)
- One study demonstrated that those who were unhappy in their marriage when first surveyed, but remained married, were likely to have an improved relationship and be happier five years later than those who divorced.(Anderson, 2014)
- Reducing the household income.(Anderson, 2014)

■ Weakening the family structure. (Anderson, 2014)

Considering this, I wonder how many divorced women have considered reconciliation? Of course, there are abusive and damaging relationships you should never reconsider. However, single women everywhere will tell you, the grass isn't greener over here. If reconciliation isn't possible, then saddle up and continue taking the journey.

Baby Mama (his)

You could be dating a man with major baby mama drama. Let's be honest, there are some good men that make bad choices. They were involved with horrible women and had children with them. Now they must deal with them for the rest of their lives. If he is still a little bitter about their breakup, this relationship could interfere with your present relationship. Just do one thing ladies. Nothing! Don't have an opinion about how he should handle his children or his ex. If you choose to stay with him, be a listening and supportive ear and let him deal with her.

Remember, whether you are in the picture or not, he must deal with her. Don't add fuel to the fire by blasting her on social media or answering his phone and letting her have it. That's not your place, they are not your children, and this is not your issue. You are dating this man; you are not married or engaged yet. Don't entangle yourself too far in those types of affairs unless the relationship warrants it, or he asks you to. Most men won't.

15

Just Friends

L et's all brace ourselves before we delve into the potpourri of friends! Are you just getting back in the dating game from long-term relationships or marriage? You need to know, that a lot has changed from the days of writing your phone number on a piece of paper one day, and a guy asking you to be his girlfriend, the next. In all seriousness, this must be the #1 issue with modern relationships. Back in the day, you met a guy, and you went on a date, (yes, a date, not hanging out, kicking it, or chilling). The man told you upfront that he had a romantic interest and a very short time later, the relationship was official, and you all were "together." Well thanks to social media, the framework of romantic relationships has drastically changed over the past few years.

Platonic Friends

No romantic interest at all

Yes, it's possible to have a male friend who is nothing more than that. This person cannot be someone you have dated or had a romantic involvement with at any time. It doesn't mean the person is not attractive. You all just don't see each other in that way. You will probably address him as "bro" or brother. Side note: never, I mean never; address a man you have a romantic interest in as "bro" it's something you can't walk back! You all are good friends and share relationship stories, and you laugh and hang out. Let me quantify this "hanging out" if you are seeing a platonic friend often, there are perhaps some underline feelings going on. Men don't spend time with their platonic female friends on a regular basis. Nothing will ever happen beyond friendship. Being platonic friends means there is no attraction on either side. If there is an attraction on either side, that is another category of friend. This is the truest definition of a friend.

Hot Friend

A friend you secretly crush

This is a male friend or acquaintance that you find attractive, yet he has not pursued anything romantic. You both may flirt a little bit, but nothing has happened. You have a secret crush on him, and it may seem obvious, he may be crushing on you as well. I think this is a great relationship to have, initially. A friendship is bonding and forming and nothing else. You have a great male friend but, one day there may be a green light to explore more. I think the art of friendship has been broken. Too often, we as women feel that if the man isn't trying to take us to the bedroom, that on some level, he is not attracted to us. That is the furthest thing from the truth. A man who is serious about you is not necessarily in a rush. He wants to take his time to get to know you and how you operate. You have time to do the same. This is actually a great place to be, but not for too long! Allowing this friendship to linger with an unspoken desire can lead to confusion. At some point, one of you needs to speak up, or live with possible regrets!

Friends with Benefits (FWB)

Sex

The bottom line, this is a no-strings-attached sexual relationship. You may hate me ladies, but I must say this; these men are not your friends. In my observation, the term "jump-off" has been replaced with FWB. It makes women feel better for only being a sexual object to a man. Sorry ladies, I must call this for what it is. It's a pseudo-relationship for you. I will never be convinced that a woman is happy at being just sex for a man. Remember ladies, these men are not your friends, involved in your life, or are there for you emotionally. Let's stop calling these "partners," friends. Women (foolishly) in my estimation, take on a faux masculine persona, to defend their FWB relationship. She does this under the guise that she also just wants sex. Hog Wash!

Talk to each of these women, you will find they are either exhausted from trying to find love, broken-hearted, lonely, or have just settled for this type of attention from a man. Ladies, there is no way around it! There is no commitment in place. This can be a very dangerous place to be, especially if a woman has entered this agreement in hopes of landing a long-term relationship. Honey, your chances of doing that became slim to none, when you allowed a man into your sacred parts, with nothing else required of him. He is probably sleeping with other people as well. Girl, if you think being a friend with benefits is going to get you to the altar faster, you need to have several seats. Could it turn into more? Of course! Anything is possible, but the likelihood is slim. Why settle? Why give your everything, and get nothing in return? The bottom line, *casual sex is never casual.* Even a potential new mate, may be turned off by your cavalier attitude about sex. No one wants a person who gives themself away "casually". It lowers your value. Is this the type of relationship you want your children to have or to see you have? Think deeply about why you are in an FWB situation with a man; what are the actual benefits you are receiving? Might not be worth the cost ladies, choose wisely.

Couple-ly

Just "hanging out" really

You met a great guy and hit it off and start seeing each other on a regular basis. You go to your favorite restaurant and a couple of his old classmates are there. As they leave out, he greets them and exchanges pleasantries. You stand there, smiling, happy to be with your man. Then, he hits you with, "This is my friend, Stacy." Suddenly, that toothpaste commercial smile fades into a resting b#### face and you are truly feeling some type of way! If this happens, there are two things to ask yourself:

- Has our relationship been defined?
- Have we talked about exclusivity?

If the answer to either of these is yes, then you need to have a talk with your man about why he didn't introduce you as his lady, girlfriend, or even just by name, for that matter. Don't make it a huge deal, but this is something you need to discuss. Remember, men hold on to their bachelorhood at all costs, so don't get too offended.

If the answer is no, then you are his friend! Ladies, it does not matter if you are seeing this man on a regular basis, and if are you are doing couples' things. If the relationship has not been defined, and you all have not talked about exclusivity, you are technically friends. I know! This modern wave of dating is much more than a notion; it's a headache. It's too much to keep up with. It's complicated! But please know the rules. You should never do "couple-ly things" without being a couple, and I'm talking about much more than just sex. If a man has not made you his woman, don't act like you are. In this time of hanging out, you should enjoy his company, nothing else. Save yourself some heartache and disappointment. Don't settle for being a friend when what you really want is a man. Yes, settling lowers your standards. Don't do it!

That One Chick...

If he discusses her often, she's more than a friend

Let's not be naïve. Men have a few friends "around" most of the time. Unfortunately (for the other party), these relationships can be disposable, should the right one come along. That right one might be you. However, if you find your guy mentioning a certain "friend" all the time, you can bet your bottom dollar, she's much more than a friend. He will casually bring up what his friend said or did, all the time. He will do this unconsciously. She may be active on his timeline. I'm not suggesting going full accusatory on him. But girlfriend, you should probably get clarity, *on that one chick*, he's always referring to.

The main thing with these crazy "friends" situations is communication. Talk, talk, talk, and talk! If you are friends, define it. Draw the lines and leave them in place. Please know that friends never mean a relationship or exclusivity. But could a friend relationship lead to more? Absolutely. Just be cautious that if someone labels you a friend, be just that. If they want more benefits, have them take it to a more exclusive level. For some, that would mean a verbal commitment. For others, that means putting a ring on it. In the meantime, enjoy your friends. Know that they are seeing other people as you should be.

Remember, you aren't doing *couple-ly* with friends, keep that barrier in place. Never settle if you want more and if you happen to catch feelings or are confused, talk about it. Yes, this is the world we live in now!

16

Friend Zone Hell

> "If you are to find true love one day, you must be cautious of
> how you handle others."

Over the last few years, a term has become very popular: the *friend zone*. The friend zone is that sweltering abyss that people are banished to for an eternity of misery. In this chapter, we will interchangeably discuss being friend-zoned, and being the friend zoner, so to speak. Please understand the difference between being *friend-zoned* and having a friend as previously described. Someone in the friend zone, at one time, attempted to date or pursue a romantic relationship. For whatever reason, the other party was "turned off" by some action, gesture or the person just didn't "do it" for them. However, they still stay in contact with them.

Ladies, we do this a lot. The friend zone captive lives in a torture chamber of sorts. What they want is right in front of them. They share good times and bad times, and they are that shoulder to cry on. Just when they think their captor has change of heart, they tighten the key on the cell! In a nutshell, you have feelings for a man that doesn't feel the same and you just "play along" like you are okay with being friends. Ladies, we do this a lot to men! Terrible, isn't it? The friend zone is not a good place to be. So how do people get there, and what are the categories of friend zones?

I Don't See Him Like THAT

This is a slightly tainted version of the platonic friend. In this scenario, one person has expressed romantic interest, but the other person "doesn't see them like that." The difference between this and the friend zone is; the initial interest or attraction was there with friend zone captives, the *I don't see them like that friend*, you wouldn't give the time of day. HOWEVER, you are aware they are smitten with you. The reverse can happen as well. You ever had a good person in your life, but you just weren't *feeling them?*

Men complain all the time that a woman wants a good man, but say, "He's just a friend." There are two sides to this coin. Ladies, we could be passing up the man of our dreams. You can depend on him, more than the men you date. You are not interested in this man whatsoever, and never will be. You hold the key, but you don't have to torture him. Holding this friend captive in the abyss is wrong because you know he will never have a chance at being with you. So, unlock the chamber and set them free. End of story ladies!

Next Lifetime!

You want them, and they may want you. However, they are committed, or maybe you are. This is really a sticky situation. There could be mutual attraction, and I would caution against staying friends with this person. It's not healthy, and you are playing with serious fire. If you have a "friend" but there is chemistry, and one or both parties is committed, make your escape swiftly. Until you find yourselves both single again, I suggest you take the advice of Ms. Badu and see them NEXT LIFETIME.

Wait for It

One of the most frustrating friend zones is the friend that is not ready to go there yet. All the elements of a great relationship are there. You click. You get along. This person is a great friend but is just not ready. This is beyond frustrating and can be downright confusing. Since feelings are there, you get mixed signals from this person and rays of hope every now and then.

However, this can turn toxic. It's like teasing a caged rabbit by dangling a carrot in its face. Be true to yourself. Don't let him put you in a holding pattern. Entertaining being a *friend-in-wait*ing, shows you are putting someone else's needs in front of your own. In contrast, if you know a man is feeling you and you are not ready for whatever reason, set him free. Don't stay in communication with him and leave the door open. Don't do it! Let me be clear, there is no romantic relationship or sex involved with any of these friends except the "friends with benefits".

Plan B

Plan B friends are options. The difference between the Plan B friend and the " *don't see them like that friend* is, you would connect with Plan B when all else fails, the latter, you would never! This man will spend money on you, buy you gifts, and you can call him when your car goes down. But you don't like him. Question? How would you feel if you found out you were a man's Plan B? This relationship is wrong, and it speaks to your character. People deserve love, not false hope. If you are to find true love one day, you must be cautious of how you handle others. Many women justify these relationships. Women feel if the man is aware her feelings aren't mutual, but he chooses to be around anyway, that's on him. There is no justification in this, stop it, cut this man off completely. These men are your Plan B because after serial dating and nothing materializes, he is your last resort in a relationship. Funny thing is, what if this was really meant to be your first option? I digress...

Sis! You Messed Up

Can't beat around the bush. Girl, you had a good one, a real good one. You simply messed it up! No way around it. Either you didn't treat him right, dismissed him, cheated on him, or you simply didn't recognize, he was literally the one God had for you. You realize it now. You all are still connected in some way, shape, or form. He may have moved on, and you feel it's no hope. Don't lie to yourself or let anyone lie to you. There is not a sea of good men that will treat you right. Everyone is not replaceable. The problem is, we have heard that so much, we believe it. We believe we can miss the mark, wait, do things our way and things will just work themselves out. No, it won't. You may need to eat a slice of humble pie, apologize, and unlock that Friend Zone cell...

Free at Last! Escape the Friend Zone

Is it possible for your captor to unlock the cell and release you from the friend zone? You should ask! It's not hard. Tell him you would like to explore more than just friendship and ask how they feel about it. Men and women both like direct contact. We don't like guessing, innuendos or clues. Could you get shot down? Yes, of course. But be ready for it. Could it make the friendship odd? For a little bit. Be warned, your friend could possibly put some distance between you and him. Make sure it's worth it and if your feelings are strong, it's worth it!

On the flip side, someone you have friend-zoned could ask you to release him. Why not explore? You only have one life to live and who knows, your friend zone captive could just be the love of your life!

17

Pick-me-sha

> "A pick-me-sha seeks any type of attention they can get, even if they must purchase it."

I t's a hot summer day. Not just any heat, but desert in Arizona summer heat. Your heart pounds, and the sweat from your forehead is dripping like a leaky faucet. You have no shades or hat, just the blistery desert sun beating down on your body relentlessly. The longer you walk, the more desperate you get for some water. At first, you wanted a big, tall glass of ice water. But now you will settle for lukewarm water from someone's hands. Yes, you are dying of thirst, and you just want some man to "pick you." *Pick-me-sha* is the new lingo for a woman who is *thirsty* and *thirsty* is the vernacular for *desperate*.

That's how some women are with men. What's interesting about pick-me-shas is, they don't know they're thirsty. They are braggarts. They talk all the time about what they have, their accomplishments, and what a good catch they are. Not to mention, she can do somersaults in bed. Pick-me-shas are the worst on social media. They claim to be wife material, insist they won't settle, and they are happy being single. They post a selfie every hour on the 2s. Well, if you are happy, you don't have to say it; just be it!

If you are a pick-me-sha, you can't hide it, because you seek attention. Pick-me-shas don't know how to just relax and take it easy. Your every conversation or post is about relationships. This is a sure sign of a pick-me-sha. You aggressively go after men, without a hint or inkling of a clue, that the men aren't interested.

A pick-me-sha seeks any type of attention they can get, even if they must purchase it. But if you just take some time and really work on yourself, you will realize, that you don't have to advertise those qualities. Yes, confidence is sexy. Confidence is loving the skin you are in. Once you understand that, before long, a man or two will be picking you!

18

Dating Matrix

If a man is confused, hesitant, or unsure, then he either may not be ready to be exclusive, or he just doesn't want to be exclusive with you.

There are stages of dating! In today's modern dating world, there seem to be no logical steps. The modern dating cycle is a concoction of confusing, friends-ish, blurred lines, non-committal, doing couple things, but not an official couple, mixed signals, Hodge Podge of mess! Exclusive relationships aren't exclusive, and it seems we get stuck somewhere in that confusing matrix, waiting to get out. But we never do!

Intimacy

You have been there, done that, got the t-shirt, matching hat, shoes, and jacket. You dove head-first into a romantic and sexual relationship and got caught up in feelings. Things crash and burn when you realize you have nothing in common with this person. Why? You never took the time to get to know them. I can't stress it enough. Slow down! Take time to get to know this person, not their bedroom skills! During this time, it's perfectly normal that you are getting to know other people if you want. Everyone does not like to date multiple people and that's fine. In this phase, there should be no sex! Get to know the person for who they are. What makes them tick? What are their dreams and aspirations? Not wet dreams! But goals, passions, and vision for their life. Girl, you can't do that if your time together consists of getting your back blown out...

Exclusivity

After a period, you all will decide if you want more. You will decide if you no longer want to see other people and have an exclusive relationship. Here is where the confusion comes in. If you don't have this talk, even if you decide to be intimate, you are still friends. We covered this earlier, but it is worth repeating. If a man is confused, hesitant, or unsure, then he either may not be ready to be exclusive, or he just doesn't want to be exclusive with you. It's fine. You should have other friends you are seeing, and you can choose to continue seeing this man or not. But if he tells you the relationship is going nowhere, take it for what it is. Chalk it up and move on. I know. Another one bites the dust.

Engagement

After exclusivity, of course, what most women want is to get engaged and married. This is where the matrix cycle comes in! By engaged I mean with a ring and a wedding date, not just a verbal proposal.

Enter the Matrix

You're stuck in the cycle of getting to know you, friends, relationships, and then...crickets! This can be downright torture! Most women are just ready to get married. Most women want to be secure. Most women don't want to continue dating with no end in sight. Most women date with marriage in mind. Never forget, it's a marriage that you want. For the man in your life, he must see you as wife material for him! Let's remember that. All men aren't players, either.

When a man sees a woman that he wants to make his wife, he will go after her with everything in him. But if he is unsure about you or is just not ready, there is nothing that you can do to settle him down. This is where you must guard your heart, know boundaries, and don't act like a wife if you are not. You must know that if you are in the first friend stage with a man, and he seems to want no more than that from you, then it is what it is.

Don't waste any more energy on trying to force the relationship because eventually, you will end up resenting him. Stop wasting your energy and let that man be your friend. Find a guy that wants more, but please, don't make any more investments with nothing in return.

19

Investments

> "Look at every relationship as an investment. It's an investment in time, and you can't get time back."

If you seem to be constantly stuck in the confuse-a-ship matrix (and it usually ends badly), don't look at it negatively. He wasn't the one. You were saved from what could have been a terrible marriage. Now, if you are making investments as a wife, you can't get mad when he doesn't make you, his wife. You need to define what an exclusive relationship means to your partner. If he expects sex and you are not giving up the cookies, let him know. He is either going to run or respect that.

Women are nurturers by nature. We are helpers—not just to our men—but in general. We don't have an off switch we can use to stop helping a man if he doesn't put a ring on it. So, what do we do? We dive head-first into the pool and entrench ourselves in our men's lives. We involve ourselves with his family, his children, work, his problems, cooking, cleaning and let's be real, for most women, sex! We give our hearts freely, in hopes that he will give it back. In some cases, these relationships will turn into a marriage. The man will love and appreciate the woman you are, and he will want to make you his own for life. But what happens to so many women, they give and give and give and not only get nothing in return, but the man they give to for years goes and gets someone else.

People say, "Why should he buy the cow when he can get the milk for free?" Listen, we need to just be real. Men buy cows every day because that cow has some valuable milk! But at the same time, you must put up boundaries. You must know when you are giving of yourself and getting nothing in return. I am not saying put a time limit on a relationship. I don't believe in that. But you do have to say to yourself, "How long am I going to give him everything he wants, and not get what I want?" That causes imbalance and frustration.

> Look at every relationship as an investment. It's an investment in time, and you can't get time back. It's almost like investing in the stock market. You pick a stock and invest in it. Then, you watch it go up or down. Some stocks just go down in value. Do you sell it, or wait for it to get better? It's up to you. It's all a gamble. If the price gets too low, you should either sell, trade, or invest elsewhere!

20

Ms. Independent

"Women will say they need their hair and nails done before they say I NEED A MAN"

"I don't need a man. I don't need a man for anything. Now I want a man, but I got this." Okay, you go girl! Let's imagine this for a moment. You are in the grocery store. Your five-year-old approaches you and says, "I don't need a mom. I don't need a mom for anything. I can get my own juice box and hot dogs. I want a mom, but I don't need one." Women will say they need their hair and nails done before they say I NEED A MAN! What's crazily ironic is, you really need one, and badly! But you want to show men that you have it together and that you are not a needy, thirsty female or pick-me-sha. Well, if you don't need a man for anything, why would he want to be in your life?

Women, you never hear a man say that he doesn't need a woman. Saying you don't need a man means you don't need a father for your children. You don't need a protector and a provider. You don't need a leader. You don't need God's design for the family. Yes, I was a single mother, raised by a divorced mother. I didn't have help from any man raising my children. Did I need a man? Yes, I did! I needed a man to be there for my girls, to help me raise them and to protect them. I needed a man to show them how a man should treat them. I needed a man to ease the load of life financially and mentally because I was drained. I needed a man!

As independent women, we do what we must do to make it. It doesn't mean that we stop living or raising our children, and it doesn't mean I was a mother and a father to them. I don't have male organs and I am not a man. I don't know how to be anything but an extraordinary mother (please stop wishing women a Happy Father's Day). Listen, I get it. I raised my children, worked in corporate America, and built many businesses, ventures, and projects. But never will you hear me say the words, "I don't need a man."

My independent sisters, continuously stating that you don't need a man is going to get you just that, NO MAN. Humans need to be needed. How would you feel if your friend, your parents or even a man said they didn't need you? Women like that, stay single for a long time and then complain that men are intimidated by their success. No, they are not. They don't want your drama and all your hostile aggression, which has taken away from your femininity.

Femininity means soft, loving, nurturing, vulnerable, and open. Girl, no man wants to date another man! Now hold up! I'm speaking of energy. Men are aggressive, and men are protectors and providers. A man wants to be able to give to his woman. And if he feels as though, you don't need him for anything, then why would he apply for the job? I mean, can he fix a cabinet, a flat tire, something? Let him be the man in your life. If you play the role, that you can do anything for yourself, then date yourself. Stop it!

For the independent female "boss" women falsely think men are intimidated by them. No, they are repelled by your masculine energy in the relationship. You may not even be aware of what you are doing. If your guy is talking about a client, project, or situation, talk to him! Don't bring up your experience, don't give him advice or offer to help unless he asks. There is a time and a place for everything. Let him have his moment. When you are with your man, he is the man. Don't be the CEO with him. It's not about diminishing your shine. It's understanding, how important it is, that he shine for you.

For men, a lot of times, they don't know how to deal with female bosses. They don't understand that we need love, security, compassion, and support. I recall a guy I was seeing a while back, didn't get me anything for Valentine's Day. I was shocked and upset. When I told him about it, he said, "I didn't know you were that type of girl." I said, "What type of girl is that?" He said, "The type of girl that liked those things." I was shocked. I assured him that I liked gifts, chocolates, and teddy bears.

Lady bosses need love, too! I am not saying turn your shine down on your accomplishments. But know the difference between a board meeting and a date. A man is not trying to hear a list of your references and business contacts. He doesn't want to feel like he is competing with you. He would much rather look in your eyes and at your smile. He'd much rather see if he can help you solve a problem.

> Femininity does not mean weakness, and it's a shame society has taken away the most powerful thing that a woman has. It's not your resume, your degrees, or your accomplishments. While admirable, your most powerful asset is that you are a woman!

21

Date Like a Girl

> "Women desire a "manly man" yet expect him to communicate and understand like a woman."

M en and women do not communicate alike. In fact, we are planets, worlds, and galaxies apart. It's a tragic mistake, so many women expect men to talk, act and react as she does. Women desire a "manly man" yet expect him to communicate and understand like a woman. Oxymoron, isn't it?

This gap in communication often leads to a decline of what could have been a good relationship. Let's make it easy for you. Men are givers, and women are receivers. Men empty out, and women take in (no pun intended with the visuals). But today, it seems as though the roles have been reversed. However, the type of quality man you desire should fully understand who he is. He understands that he is the giver and protector. He understands that he is also the hunter. So how does this work when dating? Glad you asked!

The Aggressor

If you have been talking to a man for some time, and he has not asked you out on a date, should you leap out there and ask him? You could, but I highly recommend against it. A man knows what he wants, and it will never be a guessing game. It is not necessary to ask a man on a date because, if you do, you upset the natural balance of things. I'm not saying that this is a hard and fast rule. Of course, women have put themselves out there and asked a man out, and things turned out great. But it's a way you can hint and suggest without force. Remember ladies, men absolutely hate to be forced and pushed into anything. They hate pressure. Men like for things to flow naturally and easily. If he feels like you are pushing him, he will automatically "ghost" you. Men are slow. Let's face it, ladies. We are fast-paced creatures.

We really want to skip the whole dating process and just call David Tutera to plan our dream wedding. We want to skip the whole relationship thing because it's not necessarily the man we want. We want what that man can give us! Men want relationships (let that sink in)! If you are the one, they are considering for marriage, they are going to really get to know you, which is something women should start doing. But because we put this type of pressure on a suitor, it automatically forces him to not pursue you any further. Constantly applying pressure and being forceful and aggressive (even with a soft girly voice) is very much masculine energy. This is cool for a passive man, not the Kings you claim you want.

Intentional Dating

I was looking at a post on social media that garnered thousands of responses. It simply asked, "What do you ask on the first date?" I was mortified by the answers and quickly knew, these ladies probably don't get to second dates. On the first date, you aren't asking about five-year goals, you aren't asking who he's dating (you read that right), you aren't asking about his last relationship. I would think prior to the date, you've had a few conversations for basic information, like marital status. Upfront, before the date, you must express to the man, you are dating for the purpose of marriage. Do not skip, nor downplay this. For goodness' sake, don't say you want to be married *one day*; or "I'm in no rush" (so to speak). Like a King, a Queen knows what she wants and won't settle. He needs to know according to your family values and what you want in your life, marriage is vital. Every man we polled, agreed, this is important for a woman to convey. Side note: You can't make that statement and your behavior screams anything but the *wife.*

If the man communicates that's not where he is, during the phone conversation, bid him *adieu.* If he responds to the topic of marriage with, "One day" or "Let's go with the flow," or "Let's see where it goes," put your red flags up. Remember, to be led by a man, you need to know where he is leading you. If this man isn't sure he wants marriage, you should be sure not to waste your time. You do not need another male friend. Could he lie and say something different? Of course, but if you follow the I NEED A MAN guide, you will be closing the lid on the cookie jar and girlfriend duties until the relationship is solidified. Not in word, indeed, with patience. Yes, you must be friends with a man, but not for the sole purpose of being his friend. I must bring some balance, saying you want marriage with an *attitude,* or in *desperation,* both send the wrong energy. Be calm, cool, collected. You know, be a girl! See how easy that was ladies? We think we found a better system, but it turns out, our grandmothers were right!

First Date

While on the date, be a girl! Let him open the door, park your car, and pull your seat up. Let him order your food! Give him your order and let him tell the waitress. Men like these little things. Let him take control. Let him be the man! Relax, girl! He's got this. Never, ever talk about the bill or tips. Don't touch it, and you don't bring it up. Don't mention it. A man will look at the bill, pay it and leave a tip. You do, however, thank him for the evening and a good time. During the date, listen and go with the flow of the conversation. Don't talk too much about anything depressing or traumatic. Smile, be flirty, cute, and fun! Be a girl! But please, be yourself. Don't pretend to be something you are not. That is

true man repellent! Don't overcompensate! Make sure you look naturally gorgeous, smell great, and smile!

After the Date

It's perfectly fine, after the date, if you text or call him to let him know
you enjoyed yourself. Beyond that, please let the next communication
come from him. This is not a game. It's just learning the ebbs and flows
of communication in the "get to know you" phase. It's learning how this
man communicates. If he calls you immediately that night or the next
day, that doesn't mean he really likes you. It may mean he is ready to
pounce on you like a lion in the jungle.

Men's Poll

We conducted a poll with our group of men. The question was simple,
after the first date, if you are interested in a woman, when will you
reach out? An overwhelming majority of the men said, the same night,
no later than the next day or 24 hours. Side note: the men in the poll
added, if the guy takes days to call you back, he's not interested.

Ghosted

You thought the date went well, you texted him to thank him for the
date, and he may or may not respond. However, should you not hear
from him, please do not make another call, text, or email. Don't poke
him on Facebook. Don't send sweet messages. Ladies, please simply do
nothing. If you never hear from him again, no matter how great you
thought the date was, he is not interested. If he calls, but calls later than
expected, proceed with caution as the men suggest. However, don't grill
him, he's not your child and you all aren't an item. Use your best judgment.

Stop Pursuing Him!

I truly believe that when dating, the woman should allow the man to do most of the calling and date planning in the beginning. If you are constantly the one reaching out, making plans, and sending sweet nothings, you have given the man no room to win you. Men are competitive by nature, if you do all the hunting, you've taken away his natural hunter instinct. Ladies, this is a turnoff. Girl, if a man wants you, you never have to guess or feel confused. His indecision is a decision! Remember, that the man is the giver, and the woman is the receiver and nurturer. But oftentimes, we end up being the giver. We give and give until we give out. Then, we get upset at the man for not reciprocating. You chose to do all the work. You chose to be the giver. You chose to pursue. You chose to do what he is supposed to be doing. Do you know why?

Rushing

You don't want to go through the dating phase. You just want to get to the commitment. This very fact is keeping many women single. Men sense that you are not easy going and he feels the pressure. Therefore, so many men "ghost" you for apparently no reason, so you thought. A man that cares about you wants you to be happy. He wants to do things for you. But it must be on his timing. We are so used to men rushing! They rush into a relationship and then rush into bed. After all the rushing, we crash and burn from sheer exhaustion. It's different when a man takes his time to get to know you, the real you. If you think talking to a man all day, equates to a good or quality man, you couldn't be more wrong. Many times, it's these types that are the worst. They know how to play the game and play it well.

Communication

Yes, it seems complicated. That's only because most women judge a man's communication patterns with their own. If you continue to date a man, you will find his communication may seem like it's all over the place. Let me be clear, inconsistency is not acceptable, but understanding how a man communicates is vital. Men need space, silence, and alone time to think. Women, for the most part, don't require as much. Do you know how many women have sabotaged relationships, because a man didn't communicate on her level? More than you may realize. Every absence doesn't denote he is with another woman. However, what if he is? Are you exclusive or just dating? Are you dating other people as well? Here we go with rushing again! Putting the relationship at a stage it has not yet advanced. This also shows you aren't ready. You aren't stable and emotionally mature enough to have a boyfriend, much less a husband.

Ladies, if you know how to make a good man's world peaceful, he will do anything for you. Many of you feel *doing*, things for him, shows you are a good woman. No, ma'am, that's what you think, not what he requires. *Doing* is masculine, the opposite of what your man needs. Your man needs to know you are proud of him and admire him. He needs to know verbally; you appreciate him being in your life and you find him attractive. Yes, men need to hear this. That's it, ladies. That's what he needs. That's his language. By chance, if he asks for your help with something, do it. Side note: we are talking about the beginning of the dating phase, of course, the relationship will entail much work from both parties.

In the beginning, stages, if you don't learn how a man communicates, if you don't understand how to be a girl, it will frustrate you and, in turn, frustrate him. Turn the tables, change your language, watch how it changes your outcome!

22

Waiting on My Boaz

"Was Boaz looking for her? No, but Ruth had a plan and got her man, honey!"

W e are taught to go after everything we want. We are taught that if you don't go after it, you won't get it. If you want a job, will it fall in your lap just by waiting, hoping, and praying? No! You must let employers know you are available for the position. You must put yourself out there in the job market. Sure, you can meet your future mate by just going about your everyday routine, but you still must be ready. You still must know that anywhere you go, at any time, you could meet him. You should look good and smell good. Smile and make eye contact, and let the men know that you are available! I know you're saying, "Wait, Vanessa!" You just told us to let the man pursue us?" Exactly, but let's talk about being in position to be seen and pursued!

Get in Position

"I'm waiting on my Boaz!" has become a popular saying. I really wonder who has taken the time to even read that story and know exactly what happened. While this is not a Sunday School lesson, grab a Bible or go online and look up the Book of Ruth and read it. In short, after being widowed, Ruth vowed to stay with her mother-in-law, Naomi, even after her husband's death (Ruth 1:15-18). After traveling to Naomi's native land of Bethlehem, Naomi told Ruth about an available, very rich bachelor in her family named Boaz. Ruth then requested of Naomi that she be allowed to go to his field and glean ears of grain (Ruth 2:2). Naomi gave her instructions and her blessing. She believed Ruth would find favor with him.

Ruth finds Favor

And sure enough, Boaz noticed her and promised:

- She could glean in his field anytime.
- He promised her that no men would harm her (protector).
- He opened his water supply to her, which he had in abundance (provider). Furthermore, he wanted her to look after the other women in the field (promotion).

That sounds like *favor* to me (Ruth 2:8)! But it doesn't stop there!

Wise Counsel

After Ruth told her mother-in-law about Boaz showing her favor, a light bulb came on! Naomi knew where Boaz would be that night. This wise woman instructed Ruth to get herself ready, look nice and instructed her to lie at his feet (Ruth 3:1-5) where he was resting. When Boaz discovered she was there, he requested that she stay until the morning (Ruth 3:13-14). Now, I don't know what all took place during that night; it doesn't say.

Ruth got her MAN

But whatever happened, Boaz immediately started the process, so that he could rightfully marry Ruth (Ruth 4:10). Long story short, the term "waiting on my Boaz" is quite an oxymoron. Ruth did anything but wait! She, along with Naomi, had a plan to get her man! Was Boaz looking for her? No, but Ruth had a plan and got her man, honey! She went after him, subtly, softly, and quietly. Might I add, she had the council of an older wise woman.

Your Circle

Ladies, you must surround yourself with married women, if you seek to be a wife. A few of those women should have at least twenty years of marriage experience. This is vital. It was Naomi that guided Ruth into the arms of her Boaz. Naomi was key in this union. Why we go it alone, without talking to women who have weathered these storms, is a mystery. If most of your circle of girlfriends are single or in casual relationships, most likely that's where you will remain. I don't suggest dumping friends, I suggest changing your environment and quickly.

Now, while I do believe in putting yourself out there, I personally don't believe in women approaching a man and asking him out. Do what works for you and what you are comfortable with. In our poll with the men, we asked their opinion about women asking a man on the first date. Surprisingly, most were okay with it. I would say the results were 65% for, 35% against. So according to the men (not me), go for it! I'm old school in that regard, and I'm okay with that!

For the love of Ruth, please stop saying you are waiting. Faith without action is dead. Do you want something to happen? Get up and make it happen, and take control of your love life, ladies!

23

Transparency

"When you are confident and loving you, he knows you can love him."

One of the biggest turn-offs to men is women that appear perfect. They portray an almost angelic like, unflawed, mystical being that no man can resist. Who taught you that this is what men want? A man wants a genuine, down-to-earth woman. He wants someone that loves herself and her flaws, and who's confident about who she is. That means past and present flaws and all. Think about it girl, we don't even want friends like this! When you put on a mask, it means you are hiding the real you. It means you are not proud of yourself and that you are not genuine. If you are not genuine with yourself, how can you be genuine with a man?

Ladies, if you are on a date, bragging about what a stellar individual you are, the man may say "check please." Why? He can't make a connection with you, and he won't ask you out again. Unless he is a predator and looking to take advantage. A quality man will not entertain such a woman. I can't speak enough about confidence. Ladies, it's not about your size. It's not about your looks. There is someone for everyone. We all know ladies who are married or in relationships that are not what society would consider "attractive". Yet, they have men that love them.

This doesn't mean telling all your business the first date, either. Please, don't do that. But for instance, if education comes up in conversation, and he has a master's degree, be honest and let him know that you didn't finish your bachelors. Don't be ashamed of it. If the relationship develops and you all start talking about serious financial matters, be honest: "My credit is not the best, but I'm working on it." Don't wear so much makeup that he can't see your face. Let him see the real you. When you are confident and loving you, he knows you can love him.

If you are open with him, you make him comfortable to do the same. This works for any relationship. Transparency breeds transparency. And you can only be transparent when you are comfortable, confident, and loving the skin you're in!

24

Step Out the Box

"Let things unfold naturally, you may see that the person you said you would never date, is the perfect one for you!"

Chances are if you are reading this book, you are single. You're not really dating anyone, and you're anxiously ready to meet that special person. And yes, I said anxiously. I'm so tired of society making women feel that wanting companionship or marriage is needy. That is some backward psychobabble. Life is better when you have someone to share it with, someone to go through good and bad times with, and someone to just be there to hold you when you need it. Everyone wants a constant source of love and support. This isn't my idea, it's God's. Never allow people to tell you they know better than God!

One thing is standing in the way for many of us. We fail to step out of the box, step away from the familiar and try something different. Women get a pattern and routine and stick with it. Not only that, but women also tend to take the dating phase way too seriously. You should always take note of whom you are spending your time with. But sometimes, we turn down dates because, in our minds, we already have the perfect image of our soul mate. We know exactly what he looks like and it's certainly not Larry from Accounting who is interested in you! It doesn't leave room for you to just step out and have fun.

What would it hurt to explore something or someone new? Do you realize that the perfect person for you could be 500 miles away, a bit older or younger, or even a co-worker? But, because you have too many rules, restrictions, and barriers up, you will never see them. So instead of trying to make sense of everything, take a chance. Obviously, what you have been doing hasn't worked so well. Obviously, the type of person you have chosen has not worked out for you. Perhaps he is intelligent but doesn't have all the degrees behind his name. Maybe he is a great guy but has a young child and yours are grown.

How will you ever know until you get out there and test the waters? If you relax, chill out, and just enjoy the date, let things unfold naturally, you may see that the person you said you would never date, is the perfect one for you!

25

Abandon Ship!

> "Just know his indecision about you, is a decision."

S ocial media has made it so easy to explore your options, that men are not jumping on the "exclusive-ship" so quickly anymore. And yes, I blame social media. It's opened a world that was never there. It's given both men and women, access to people they never had before. Now, what they don't realize, is that most of these options are not options at all. They are simply illusions and fantasies of something that probably will never materialize. However, because of the Internet and some of our sisters lowering their standards, there are various categories of relationships. Now, girlfriend, it's completely up to you what treatment you will accept or not accept. People only treat us how we allow them to. See if you can identify yourself as being a passenger on one of these ships:

Inbox-a-Ship (IM/DM)

The infamous IM or DM, being trolled by cyber-players, looking for fresh conquest! The messaging game is savage! Basically, a man or a woman starts up a conversation with several people and chat. Some get sexual, and those conversations are preceded by sending pictures of genitalia (yuck). Some of the conversations turn romantic, and people seem to get attached and chat for hours. But rarely does it go outside of that. And remember, your messaging boo is not exclusive. The same chat he is having with you, he is having with others. Do you see that green dot on? Yes, he's chatting! You're in an inbox-a-ship if most of your communication is done inside the box, but rarely outside of it. However, your inbox boo may graduate to a:

Text-a-Ship

You've exchanged phone numbers. So now the main method of communication is via text. Morning, noon, and night. You may get a "Good Morning" text, "Thinking about you" text, or the dreaded "Hey Beautiful". Full-fledged conversations are going on, yet it's still a text-a-ship because your main mode of communication is via text. And yes, this is a major red flag!

You can't possibly build a real relationship via either of these methods. This is a cop-out to connecting with a real person. Most of the time, the person is texting or in-boxing, because they have a real relationship and cannot physically talk. Don't get me wrong. Both have their place. For the initial conversation or during work hours when you can't talk, it is fine. But if your guy texts more than he calls, sweetheart, you don't have a relationship, you have a text-a-ship. You don't get to hear their tone of voice, or how they act and react to things. You don't get to hear their environment. I strongly suggest you tell your suitor in the beginning, you appreciate real communication and would like to talk as much as possible. If he doesn't oblige, well you know what to do!

Situation-ship

This could encompass many things. For all intents and purposes, this is someone you have spent a decent amount of time with, and you seem to get along well. But for whatever reason, the relationship has not been defined, and no commitment is in place. This could also be a situation where the person is separated, or in the middle of a divorce. It's a pseudo-relationship. It looks like a real one, has the residue of a real one, but it's not. If a man does not know, who he wants you to be in his life, I suggest you be nothing until he figures it out. Preferably, find a man that knows. Situation-ships rarely turn out good. He may be a good person, and you all have a good time, but you end up with the short end of the stick, every time. In many cases, for years.

What are We-ship?

What are we? Have you asked your "guy" this or does the thought constantly swirl around in your mind? Yes? Girlfriend, you are in a full-fledged what are we-ship! This relationship or whatever it is, has so many mixed signals, red flags, and inconsistencies mixed with good moments, that you don't know what to think. Hence, the term what are we-ship. In this instance, key elements are missing, perhaps he has been to your home, but you have never been to his. Or better still he is unavailable during certain times of the day, week, or weekend.

You may have met his friends but not his children or family. But do not let that fool you either, you can have met a man's entire family and he is not sure if you are the one for him. He does nice things for you; he is a solid guy and a good catch in your mind, so you hold on. But you are not happy because you are not confident where you stand. If you have asked him the infamous "What are we" and he gave a vague answer, just know his indecision about you, is a decision. He can genuinely like you, he probably does. But, either something in his life is not conducive to him being in a committed relationship right now, or he just doesn't see you as his "wife".

What women do, is engage in sexual activity, before the relationship or commitment is established with no understanding. Somehow women feel as this should advance the relationship, in a man's mind it doesn't. You all had sex, that's it. Ladies, I can't stress how we need to stop doing this. But do not beat yourself up (just do better). What you feel like a man needs, may not be what he needs at all. Don't make these men the bad guys, simply do good to yourself and exit stage left until you find a man that is sure that he wants you in his life.

Relationship

I know right! It sounds like I cursed! But yes, relationships are still around, and they do exist. A relationship is when two people exclusively are seeing each other romantically. This should be very clear in the beginning. If you have never had the "talk," you are not in an exclusive relationship. I don't care how much you have seen each other, how much you do for each other, or how much you may have feelings for each other. An exclusive relationship is a verbal agreement. The relationship is not a secret. Now, don't start posting every millisecond of your time together as a couple (please don't). The important people in his and your lives, should know you all are together. No blurred lines, no mixed signals, no hot and cold.

Listen up ladies! If it's a relationship you want, do not settle for any of those other ships. If you're happy making $10 per hour with no benefits (no offense to anyone that does), is your salary going to miraculously jump to $25 per hour with benefits? Anything is possible, but probably not. What you settle for and agree upon is what you get. If a man doesn't want a relationship, immediately tell him in the beginning, that's what you are looking for and you don't want to waste your or his time. If he insists on just being friends, let him know that you have enough friends.

Being a man's friend when you want a relationship is settling, even if there is no sex involved. You have settled for less than what you wanted. And that my ladies, is the essence of what's wrong in these awful, modern-day, technology-driven, pseudo relationships!

26

War on Family

> The *destruction of the family agenda* has affected so many areas of life, ideals, and behaviors, that most are not aware of its influence.

U nless you are hiding under a rock, you have noticed there is an ever brewing, disdain, disgust and even demonization of the *nuclear family*, also referred to as the: *traditional family, western prescribed family,* or *patriarchal family.* Those are all catchphrases to get people programmed to believe the natural family structure, *man, woman, child,* is an outdated, near-criminal, oppressive, concept of white supremacy. For a moment, allow me to switch into my journalistic hat. I included this information in I NEED A MAN because if you desire a family, in the traditional sense, everything in the world right now is set against you. Sounds insane, doesn't it?

For the past few decades, there has been a slow burn eroding away at the fundamental element of life on earth. That burn turns women against men, turns children against parents and puts all things including private property, and the raising of children, in the hands of what they call "the state." Please do not be fooled, funding and controlling all these movements, are the same rich ruling elite class, that have controlled resources for centuries. These elite FAMILIES understand wealth is passed through family lineage. Think of anyone wealthy, you think of their family names: Rockefeller, Rothschild, Kennedy, Dupont, Bush, etc. I gather no one gave the elite wealthy class, the memo about destruction of the nuclear family. I digress.

The *destruction of the family agenda* has affected so many areas of life, ideals, and behaviors, that most are not aware of its influence. Just research for yourself, the near dismal rate of marriage, divorce and children born into single-family homes. It is absolutely staggering. So, you will be further aware, these movements are anti-capitalism. They believe no one should own private property (research on any non-Google search engine "You shall own nothing, and you shall be happy). These movements claim that women and children are the property of men. Men have families for the sole means of production which *feeds* the capitalist system. Therefore, the family unit will be destroyed, as capitalism is destroyed. (F., 1847/2020).

Oddly, they promote women to go into a workplace, that is overwhelmingly owned by elite men, where they must submit to the will of their superiors. Interesting, isn't it? Also understand, this same movement promotes abolition of religion, God, and promotes promiscuity at a level you would not believe. Please educate your daughters entering higher academia. This is where most women get these ideals planted and programmed in their minds. They will even convince you that marriage and motherhood stem from white supremacy and consensual sex with your husband is rape! It is absolute lunacy. The following is just a microcosm of the statements about the family from Feminist, Marxist, and Communist leaders, and Margaret Sanger (Planned Parenthood Founder). Sanger was a eugenicist and had an agenda to destroy the black race and reduce the population. Her methods were so effective, they were employed in Nazi, Germany. The government, and many elite foundations, still fund Planned Parenthood to this day. Review some of these absolute abhorrent thoughts on marriage, family, and childbearing.

- "But for my view, I believe that there should be no more babies." (Sanger, 1947)
- "The most merciful thing that the large family does to one of its infant members is to kill it."(Sanger, The Wickedness of Creating Large Families, 1920)
- "We don't want the word to go out that we want to exterminate the Negro population"(Sanger, Letter to Dr. C.J. Gamble, 1939)
- "Horrid word, family!" Aleister Crowley (Crowley, 1954)
- "Since marriage constitutes slavery for women, it is clear that the Women's Movement must concentrate on attacking this institution. Freedom for women cannot be won without the abolition of marriage." Sheila Cronan (Cronan, 1973)
- "Abolition of the family" (F., 1847/2020), Communist Manifesto
- "The institution of sexual intercourse is anti-feminist." Ti-Grace Atkinson (Atkinson, Amazon Odyssey, 1974)
- "The price of clinging to the enemy [a man] is your life. To enter into a relationship with a man who has divested himself as completely and publicly from the male role as much as possible would still be a risk. But to relate to a man who has done any less is suicide. . . . I, personally, have taken the position that I will not appear with any man publicly, where it could possibly be interpreted that we were friends." Ti-Grace Atkinson (Atkinson, Amazon Odyssey, 1974)
- "The objective of every feminist reform, from legal abortion to the ERA (Equal Rights Amendment) to child-care programs, is to undermine traditional family values." (Willis, na)
- Now deleted from the Black Lives Matter website, was the objective to "disrupt" the "Western-prescribed nuclear family structure." (Bernstein, 2020). The website went on to add, that they would: create an environment for mothers, children, and extended family, strangely, the word *father* was left out.
- Even behind the cloak of "climate change" is the notion that "Kids are bad for the earth, morality suggests we stop having them."(Reider, 2017)

This is such a minuscule example of the very planned long-ranged agenda, which is also been laced in primary education for nearly 100 years. Look for a project from me on this subject very soon, in the meantime, do your own research. The agenda isn't hidden at all.

Let's examine now, some practical benefits of marriage in terms of health and income:

Benefits of Marriage

- Married people smoke and drink less (Anderson, 2014)
- Married individuals have the lowest incidence of diabetes, hypertension, and heart disease (Anderson, 2014)
- Married respondents experience per person net worth increases by 77 percent over single respondents. (JL., 2005)
- Additionally, their wealth increases on average 16 percent for each year of marriage. Divorced respondents' wealth starts falling four years before divorce and they experience an average wealth drop of 77 percent. (JL., 2005)

There is a steep decline among men in desiring marriage. Due to the high divorce rate and the financial burden to men after divorce, many are forgoing the idea. Be sure to share this with any man you know that hold those sentiments:

Marriage Benefits for Men

- Married men are less likely to commit suicide than men who are divorced or separated (Anderson, 2014)
- Married men are more likely to live longer after a diagnosis of cancer, especially prostate cancer (Anderson, 2014)
- Married men live longer than men who never married. (Anderson, 2014)

- One-fourth of the older divorced men remained isolated and lonely (Anderson, 2014)
- A three-decade study concluded that "children living with their married, biological parents consistently have better physical, emotional, and academic well-being." (Anderson, 2014)

We live in a science-driven world, there is your science! Cancel culture is trying to cancel the unit that has sustained human life since the beginning of time. One would beg to ask if the nuclear family will be destroyed, what's the replacement? How will humans be born if men and women cease to procreate?

Indeed, the title of the book I NEED A MAN is a much-needed slap in the face of a society that teaches, women NEED a career, NEED an education but DON'T NEED a family or NEED a MAN. If that's your choice, no one stands in your way, but don't stand in the way of those that choose to honor our men and our families.

27

Embrace the Feminine

> Your femininity should not start and end with a man, the feminine is WHO you are and that is not circumstantial.

M odern society has taught, the traditional attributes of women are weak, and men are strong. Do not let that language deter you. Men and women are different, together, our individual traits make for a balanced union and family life. Both men and women can possess traditional masculine and feminine traits at times. This chapter will be focused on enhancing the feminine, which has become a lost art.

What are some practical ways we can be our feminine?

Show up and show out!

Men are visual, you should always look your best, for yourself! This does not mean every day, you step out with 6" stilettos and 49" hair extensions. Whether it's jeans and gym shoes, sandals and sundresses, or suits and stilettos, be fresh, hair styled, smelling good, and always smiling. Your inner presence will hit the room before you do. Your inner essence should reflect outwardly. When we as women look good, we feel good, therefore, we are more confident. So wherever you show up, make sure you show out!

Scoff desperation

We covered this before, but it bears repeating. You want to repel a good man; then act desperate. Remember he wants a prize, desperation shows you have no options. It shows you are at the bottom of the barrel. A pick-me-sha! Men are hunters, so he wants to know that when he has won you, he has a prize. You shouldn't be easily accessible to all men. Desperation screams no options, which signals low value.

Cool Girl

Girl, hear me very well on this. Men love cool, calm, and collected women. A cool girl understands her man is busy and working, and cannot text and talk on the phone all day. When he's able to talk, she doesn't badger him about not calling. She doesn't allow him to "ghost" her either because she has boundaries. She is level-headed and knows how to handle a crisis. Not to the point of being robotic, but she is rational, wise, and calm.

Boundaries

Feminine women have clear boundaries. While she is not stoic, she clearly knows when someone has no intentions of respecting her boundaries and will restrict their access to her life. Do not accept behaviors that you are not okay with to save face. That's putting another person first. A feminine woman has boundaries and men love it, it's an obstacle to them, it puts your value high. Accepting any and everything from a man, reeks of low self-confidence and that is anything but feminine.

Communication

Perchance, you've noticed your man has put some distance between you two, and you are concerned. This is extremely common for all men, so learn this quickly. Side note: Remember, men don't talk it out, they think it out. Don't force him to talk. Women talk, remember, they are not women! Here are two examples of texts that can be sent the right feminine way and the incorrect aggressive irrational way.

- Text A-"Hi babe, hope all is well. Lately, I've felt our communication has been off and it really doesn't feel great. I value our time, and this distance seems quite out of the norm for you. Let's talk when you can, I'm genuinely concerned." That's feminine. It's not accusatory nor riddled with unfounded assumptions. This text deals with her feelings and shows concern. Mature women would never dive deeper via text.

- Text B-"Seriously? Three days? I don't take kindly to being ignored. Whatever or whoever, you are doing, keep doing it. People make time for what's important, apparently, I'm not important, have a nice life." This is proceeded by several memes on social media. Do you see how immature and irrational that was? Not one concern for him, no proof of accusations. Just irrational emotions. Many women are like this. Not in the least bit wife material, more like an unhinged teenager.

Voice Tone

I cannot stress enough, that one of the top alluring qualities of a woman that can break a man's defenses down, is a calm, sweet, soft voice. This must be a conscious action. Many of us talk loud and aggressive, so you must slow down, calm down and choose your words wisely. Men will tell you; a woman's soft voice will do things to him you can't imagine.

Busy not inaccessible

A feminine woman has a life of her own and is busy. A man wants to know, in all your busyness, will you fit into his life? If you are always on the go, when will you have time for him? I hate to say it, ladies, working yourself into oblivion, staying on the grind, always working overtime, is masculine energy. As a woman, you need balance and rest. Men are practical, never forget that. He wants to be able to pamper and take care of you, and you pamper him as well. He can't do this when you are busy all the time.

Ladies, I can't express enough, no matter what society tells you, your power is and always will be, in your FEMININE. Own it and embrace it, practice it, and walk-in it daily. Change your patterns and habits and you will tangibly see your outcomes will be quite different. Sooner than you think, the man you NEED will NEED you just as badly.

28

From Ms. Independent to Mrs.

"I will only accept a MAN that sees me as his WIFE"

Ladies, we've got work to do! If a man is what you want, and a higher quality man, do not wait until he walks in the door, prepare yourself now. You can't date like you used to; as stated in the beginning of the book, erase those modern dating thoughts, it won't work for dating with marriage in mind. Here are things to do right now:

Let's Work

- Clean up your credit, pay down debts and student loans.
- If you move around a lot, get stable.
- If you are not happy with your career path, change it.
- Take a class, learn a new skill, attend a workshop.
- Get in shape, get healthy, lose weight.
- Change your eating habits, work out, buy a bike.
- Moisturize and exfoliate your skin, hands, feet, and face (men love softness).
- See a stylist, change up your look, get a new hairstyle.
- Are your financial affairs in order?
- Get life insurance, car insurance, health insurance.

- How is your home-life?
- Clean your home, I mean deep clean.
- Get rid of clutter, clean out drawers.
- Throw out the old to prepare for the new.
- For goodness' sake, fold your laundry!
- How is your spiritual life?
- Get your spiritual life back in alignment.
- Forgive and heal broken relationships.

When the life you have made for yourself is better, including the environment you live in, you will feel better. In turn, you will also attract better. Are you ready for different results, a different type of man and outcome? Yes? Then you need to make the necessary changes in your life that will be conducive and attractive to a mature, grounded, and stable man. Guess what ladies? You need to do these things anyway, for yourself! Learn to be better for your self and better men will show up. Plain and simple!

So that you have a practical guide, say this prayer every single day.

I NEED A MAN

Not just any MAN
I have experienced lots of MEN
I only desire the MAN GOD has for ME
I will no longer entertain a MAN that isn't my husband
I will no longer allow men to break my boundaries
I will no longer stay in uncertain situations
I will no longer stay where I'm not valued
I will no longer entertain a MAN who treats me as an option
I will only accept a MAN that sees me as his WIFE
I will get the necessary healing I need for this next phase

I will begin to live a better life for myself and my
family
I know that it won't be easy
I am ready for change
That change starts with ME
I forgive others
I forgive myself
Prepare my HEART
Prepare my MIND
Prepare my SOUL
Prepare my BODY
For my new LIFE as a WIFE
I will get closer to GOD
Because it's only in GOD
I'll be able to clearly see MY KING
I'm ready now to transfer
From MS INDEPENDENT to MRS!

AMEN!

THE END but really THE BEGINNING

Vanessa Lynn

Look for "I Need a Man" daily journals, a companion
booklet for Christians "Jesus is my Valentine" and "I Need
a Man" merchandise. Bring Vanessa Lynn to your city or
Book Club meeting! Vlynnbooks@pm.me

Works Cited

4 Ways Childhood Trauma Can Effect Adults. (2017, June 1). Retrieved from Psychology Today: https://www.psychologytoday.com/us/blog/mindful-anger/201706/4-ways-childhood-trauma-can-affect-adults

Anderson, J. (2014). The Impact of Family Structure on the Health of Children: Effects of Divorce. *The Linacre, 81*(4), 378-387.

Atkinson, T.-G. (1974). In *Amazon Odyssey* (p. 90. 91). Links Books.

Atkinson, T.-G. (1974). In *Amazon Odyssey* (p. 86). Links Books.

Bernstein, B. (2020, September 21). *Black Lives Matter Removes Language.* Retrieved from Yahoo News: https://news.yahoo.com/black-lives-matter-removes-language-185621063.html?soc_src=social-sh&soc_trk=ma

Cronan, S. (1973). "Marriage". In *Radical Feminism.* Harper Collins.

Crowley, A. (1954). Family Public Enemy #1. In *Magick Without Tears* (p. Chapter 52).

F., M. K. (1847/2020). Proletarians and Communists. In M. K. F., *The Communist Manifesto* (p. 52). Pathfinder Press.

Families: Single Parenting and Today's Family. (2019, October 31). Retrieved from American Psychological Association: http://www.apa.org/topics/parenting/single-parent

Ferguson, S. (2021, November 9). Retrieved from https://psychcentral.com/health/serial-monogamist

Hernandez, E. (2021, January 15). *Psychological Effects of Online Dating.* Retrieved from https://eddie-hernandez.com/psychological-effects-of-online-dating/

JL., Z. (2005). Marriage and Divorce's Impact on Wealth. *Journal of Sociology,* 406-424.

Matthews, H. (n.d.). *Online Dating and Marriage Success.* Retrieved from Datingadvice.com: https://www.datingadvice.com/online-dating/online-dating-marriage-success

Online Dating Report. (2017). Retrieved from Kaspersky Daily: https://www.kaspersky.com/blog/online-dating-report/

Reider, T. (2017, 11 15). *Science proves kids are bad for Earth. Morality suggests we stop having them.* Retrieved from NBC News: https://www.nbcnews.com/think/opinion/science-proves-kids-are-bad-earth-morality-suggests-we-stop-ncna820781

Sanger, M. (1920). The Wickedness of Creating Large Families. In *Woman and the New Race* (p. 67).

Sanger, M. (1939, December 10). *Letter to Dr. CJ. Gamble.* Retrieved from https://libex.smith.edu/omeka/files/original/d6358bc3053c93183295bf2df1c0c931.pdf

Sanger, M. (1947). (J. Parsons, Interviewer)

Summers, M. (2018). *Major League Dating.* Retrieved from Women to Avoid Dating: https://www.majorleaguedating.com/women-to-avoid-dating/

Symptoms of Childhood Trauma in Adults. (2019, January 16). Retrieved from The Treatment Specialist: https://thetreatmentspecialist.com/symptoms-of-childhood-trauma-in-adults/

U.S. Single Family Households. (2012). Retrieved from https://post.ca.gov/portals/0/post_docs/publications/Building%20a%20Career%20Pipeline%20Documents/safe_harbor.pdf

Willis, E. (na).

Zuckerman, A. (2020, May 12). *Online Dating Statistics.* Retrieved from Compare Camp: https://comparecamp.com/online-dating-statistics/ Arthur Zuckerman May 12, 2020

Directory

Directory

CPSIA information can be obtained
at www.ICGtesting.com
Printed in the USA
BVHW040529221221
624596BV00017B/1657